KELLY GROVIER

ON THE LINE

CONVERSATIONS WITH
SEAN SCULLY

For Caspar & Oisin

*... you can fashion everything
from nothing every day, and teach
the morning stars to sing ...*

William Butler Yeats, 'A Prayer for my Son', 1921

p. 1 *Adoration* (detail), 1982
p. 2 *Windows* (detail), 1980–81

First published in the United Kingdom in 2021
by Thames & Hudson Ltd, 181A High Holborn,
London WC1V 7QX

First published in the United States of America in 2021
by Thames & Hudson Inc., 500 Fifth Avenue, New York,
New York 10110

On the Line © 2021 Thames & Hudson Ltd, London
Text © 2021 Kelly Grovier
All artworks by Sean Scully © 2021 Sean Scully

Page design by Lisa Ifsits

British Library Cataloguing-in-Publication Data
A catalogue record for this book is available from
the British Library

Library of Congress Control Number 2021933064

ISBN   978-0-500-09431-0

Printed in China by RR Donnelley

MIX
Paper from
responsible sources
FSC® C144853
www.fsc.org

Contents

The Storyteller

Sean Scully's celebrated paintings of expressive stripes and blocks of sumptuous colour are at once carefully ordered and free-flowing, muscular and lyrical, guarded and brutally frank. So too is his conversation. Even the briefest of chats with Scully invariably yields a punchy phrase or two that you find yourself turning over in your mind long afterwards. That was my experience. I first met the abstract artist in Northern Ireland in 2009. He was opening a major retrospective of his work in Belfast's Ulster Museum and I was reviewing the exhibition for the *Times Literary Supplement*. The museum had just reopened its doors following a lavish refurbishment and its curators were keen to show off the institution's impressive new cathedral-sized galleries. They needed paintings that could hold their own and not be lost in all that air. Inviting Ireland's most famous living artist, whose colossal canvases belie the pinched prospects with which Scully entered the world – all but homeless on the streets of Dublin in 1945 – was an inspired and inspiring choice.

I remember sitting across from Scully in the museum's café, keen to ask him about the unique lustre of his works – how he manages to compress layers of murky paint into a smoky luminosity that seems to ember from inside. 'The way a thing is made', he memorably replied, 'is what it is.' The response, as I've come to discover over the ensuing years of close friendship, was pure Scully. His words often have an aphoristic quality to them – a philosophical elasticity that makes them resonate beyond the topic at hand. I was asking about something practical, but Scully was searching for something deeper. He always is.

The ragged geometries of vertical and horizontal bands that characterize Scully's abstract canvases may seem far removed

Kelly Grovier and Sean Scully

from the realm of verbal storytelling. But I soon discovered that they issue from an imagination as adept at assembling words as it is at arranging ambiguous fields of battered colour. When Scully and I met up again a few months later at a café near Shepherd Market, Mayfair, his gift for allegorical expression was on full display. He told me that he had just been invited to decorate the interior of Santa Cecília de Montserrat – a Romanesque monastery that sits atop a mountain outside Barcelona, Spain. As we talked about the project (which, now completed, has been compared with Henri Matisse's contributions to the Rosary Chapel in Vence, France, and with the Rothko Chapel in Houston, Texas), Scully recalled an episode from his childhood in south London, where his family had moved when he was four – an anecdote that, like a thousand he has shared with me since, shed unexpected light on his art and imagination.

Scully told me that, when he was a little boy, he stole from his parish church a clutch of long white votive candles, wrapped them like fish in newspaper, and buried them deep in the family garden. It was an intriguing confession, utterly precise in its detail, yet irresolvable in its symbolic meaning. He recalled that a gentle and forgiving priest eventually visited his house and that the two dug up the liturgical loot together, like a pair of resurrection men. The memory had all the qualities of what the Romantic poet William Wordsworth would call in his autobiographical epic *The Prelude* a 'spot of time': a moment of adolescent transgression that, exalted by the fructifying power of imagination, shaped the growing boy's soul. As Scully poetically recalled the strange burial and disinterment of those waxen bones, I couldn't help wondering if that curious ritual, all those years ago, wasn't somehow connected with the inscrutable incandescence I sensed smouldering beneath the surface of his paintings, as if a secret source of light lay hidden deep inside them that ceaselessly gutters and glows. 'The way a thing is made is what it is.'

This is the thing about talking with Scully – the gritty adages and endless, alluring stories accumulate like brushstrokes on a living canvas. Just when you think you've discerned a defining pattern, another layer is added and another after that. The anecdotes never cohere into a finished picture. There is always something more pulsing underneath. Scully's paintings may rely on repetition, but his conversation rarely does. It's constantly new. Though he and I have met on countless occasions in London and Paris, Barcelona and Venice, Dublin and Oxford, and have spoken for untold hours on the phone or in person in cars, trains, boats and jets, discussing the mysteries of art and life, the portrait he paints of himself is forever evolving.

I wanted to capture a time-elapsed segment of that endlessly emerging picture of who Scully is. This book aims to do just that by preserving a sequence of telephone conversations that I had with the artist in the spring and summer of 2020. Against a backdrop of global anguish as the COVID-19 pandemic forced governments around the world to declare strict lockdowns, Scully and I would speak every few days, often for hours on end. Throughout our dialogue he was in New York, sheltering in place with his wife, the artist Liliane Tomasko, and their 10-year-old son, Oisin, while I was in Northern Ireland, self-isolating with my wife, Sinéad Sturgeon, who is a lecturer in Irish Studies, and our 3-year-old son, Caspar. On the line, Scully and I talked about everything. With extraordinary candour, he reflected on a remarkable range of topics, from his knockabout childhood on the streets of Dublin and London to the indelible mark he has left on contemporary art, from being rejected by nearly every art school in England to the power of love and loss in the making of enduring works. What follows is a curation of those dozens of hours of recorded conversation. Throughout, I have endeavoured to contextualize Scully's many colourful stories, observations and asides in the broader tapestry of his life, his career and the ever-unfolding story of art.

Untitled, 1966

CHAPTER ONE

Abstract Two Blues

SS My family was a shipwreck. You know, I'm the only person in my entire extended family who has studied at university. That's quite a thing, isn't it?

Scully often talks about his family and about growing up in London, having moved there from Dublin when he was four. But he rarely describes his past in the same way twice. There are always new stories to share, salvaged from childhood and adolescence. It is as if he is forever trying to find the right vantage from which to perceive how he entered the world and what, exactly, set him on his extraordinary journey to becoming one of the most important artists working today. 'I was born in Dublin, which is a dirty old town,' he wrote in a brief prose sketch in 2001 – one of hundreds of such reflections on life and art that Scully has kept over the course of his career, which shed light on his thinking from moment to moment, year to year. 'We left Dublin, my parents, my little brother and I, when I was four, before I'd had time to talk with an Irish accent... So I grew up in London (another dirty old town with a million dust-covered trees) as a phony Englishman. This, of course, resulted in discontent. My family originally was aristocratic, dispossessed by the English for having (as an excuse) the wrong religion. So I always had the feeling: "There's something wrong with this picture."' Over the course of our many conversations, I had the strong sense of speaking with someone who was ceaselessly striving to bring that picture – the picture of who he really is – into focus.

KG How did your parents react to you being the first in the family to attend university? Were they proud of you?

The Scully family, with Sean's cousins Lesley and Anna, 1949

ss I think they were befuddled by me from early on. They thought that I was not normal. They thought of me as very peculiar, I think. They never came to any of the institutions where I studied. One of them, Croydon, was a twenty-minute drive from where they lived. And the other one, Newcastle, was next to Durham, where my mother's parents lived. My grandfather was a coal miner; they were all coal miners up there. And my parents never came. I think they were somewhat disinterested and in a way, perhaps, a little resentful. I don't know.

My father had a complicated relationship with me, a competitive, dominating relationship. My mother had a very manipulating relationship. My mother was a great operator really, a dealmaker – with everything. When she was pregnant, my parents were on the run from Britain because my dad was a deserter. They couldn't get extradited from Dublin and she got fed by nuns. That's why I grew up to be so big, I guess, and she converted to Catholicism. She was a Protestant from the north of England and Scotland, and she converted to Catholicism until it didn't suit her any more. When it became inconvenient, she dumped it.

But they were basically very uninterested in these matters. These higher matters. And they were uninterested in art. It was the most peculiar thing. All my friends when I was growing up, they just didn't know what to make of me. It was as if I was in the wrong place or something. The babies got mixed up or something like that.

KG When did you first start thinking about art?

SS I remember I had a bicycle. And I'll never forget it. It was cerulean blue. And if you look at two of my early paintings, the two figurative paintings, they have cerulean blue in them.

Scully is describing a pair of canvases from 1967 – *Untitled (Seated Figure)* and *Figure in a Room* – which haver between figuration and abstraction by boldly breaking down the body's presence, muscle by shadow, into precincts of rich colour that jigsaw with the spaces they inhabit. The subjects may be seated, but they are far from motionless. They simultaneously inhabit this world and another. At once palpable and immaterial, they judder between a physicality we share with them and an elusive evanescence to which our spirits are impelled. Most impressively, perhaps, they have a look – a uniqueness of vision all their own – that is well beyond the years of the 22-year-old who authored them.

SS Cerulean blue is that lovely pale blue. I will never forget the colour of that little bicycle, a three-wheeler. I used to ride all around the Old Kent Road on my own, and make up these fantasies about where I was going. I would ride around entirely unchecked, and I was four. I remember there was a lorry parked at the end of my street – and again, I'll never forget this – it had a ladder up the side, built into it. I thought it was the most beautiful thing, and I fantasized

Figure in a Room, 1967

Untitled (Seated Figure), 1967

Three Women Bearing Arms I, 1966–67

WHAT ART IS

June 2004

I think that Art, is a wound in a
dance with love. And if the wound
and the love are the same size
they can dance well.

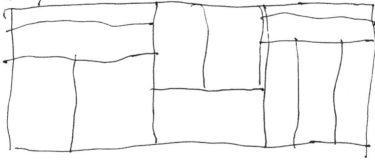

Handwritten page, 'What Art Is', 2004

Abstract Two Blues, 1965–66

about climbing up that ladder. The top of the lorry had a frame around it – you know, for extra luggage, like the old-style lorries used to have – and I had these fantasies always about climbing on the top.

At the other end of the street was the barber's pole. So, if you look at those two symbols – the ladder and the barber's pole – well, there's a career. Plus you've got cerulean blue. You've got it all there.

As Scully spoke, I was reminded of a small gouache on paper that he made between 1965 and 1966, *Abstract Two Blues*, which now seemed, in the context of his memory, to be especially important – seminal, even, as if it were the primordial soup from which so many shapes of his imagination, and particularly his later 'Landline' series of thick horizontal bands of brooding colour and highly gestural brushstrokes, would eventually emerge. I mention the parallel to him and how, in retrospect, there seems to have been a kind of inevitability about how everything would unfold.

ss I can't figure it out, actually. I just think I was touched by something.

Indeed, he clearly was. Over the course of the next half-century, Scully would emerge as one of the most important artists of his generation. He is credited with rescuing abstract art when the genre found itself in a deep crisis in the late 1970s. He 'broke the logjam of American minimalist painting', as Gillian Wearing would later describe it. But I was keen to know more about how these stars came to align in the early years of Scully's upbringing and form the curious constellation of brilliance that is Sean Scully.

KG Do you remember what it was that got you thinking about art as a viable option? Your parents weren't talking about art.

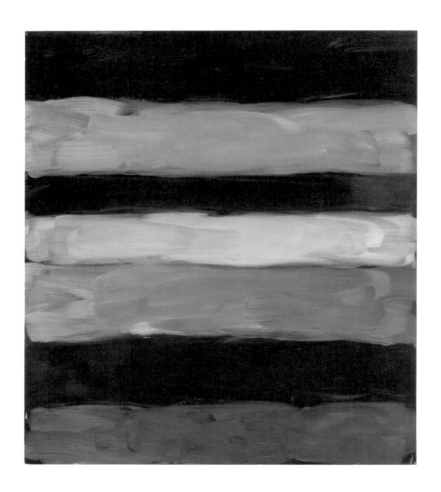

Landline Skyline, 2014

Landline Blue Veined, 2016

Vincent van Gogh, *Van Gogh's Chair*, 1888

I know you would eventually begin to visit London's Tate Gallery to look at *Van Gogh's Chair*, which had a profound influence on you and which you said 'made everything possible because it was so honest and direct'. And you spent a lot of time at the National Gallery in Trafalgar Square...

ss Yes, later, but not when we went there to feed the pigeons. We didn't give a shit about that big building. We didn't even know what it was. My parents didn't have the first idea. So, to me, it's kind of inexplicable. That little three-wheel bicycle, and the colour of it, was so fabulous. Do you remember in *Citizen Kane*...

KG   Rosebud.

SS   It's a sleigh, isn't it?

KG   Yeah, it's the sleigh that Orson Welles [playing the character
      Charles Foster Kane] remembers on his deathbed. He had
      it as a little boy. So your cerulean blue three-wheel bike,
      like 'Rosebud', came to stand for the complex innocence of
      childhood?

SS   These things are so important. They touch your heart incred-
      ibly. Then, of course, I went to the convent school. That was
      important because of some shitty Stations of the Cross
      paintings, which I would later try and find.

When Scully was a little boy he would attend Mass at an impro-
vised church called St Joan of Arc. On rainy days, the sermon
was inaudible above the racket of rain on the roof of the ersatz
structure. 'There, against that elemental hammering,' I wrote
in a catalogue published on the occasion of an exhibition of
Scully's work at Palazzo Falier, Venice, in 2015, the future artist
'traced a trajectory of torment and mystical triumph around the
room as his eyes followed the Stations of the Cross depicted
in painted panels on the humble sanctuary's makeshift walls.
Week after week, the rain's vertical drive intersected in his
imagination with the horizontal sweep of suffering and salvation as his eyes moved back and forth, from Gethsemane to the
Crucifixion; back and forth, from Judas's kiss to the soundless
tomb; back and forth, like the lash of a whip; back and forth,
like his barber father's razor on a leather strap; back and forth,
like an artist wielding a carpenter's brush. In Scully's mature
work, each shuddering stripe subsumes a stage in the soul's
movement through the cosmos. Each has its own density and
struggle. Sometimes the stripes are slow and sluggish, like a man
whose knees buckle under the shouldered weight of a crushing

beam. Sometimes they're light and evaporative, like a spirit rising through a battered stretch of blood-stained linen.' When attending his cousin's funeral as an adult, Scully asked after these crude, though important, panels.

ss There was an Irish priest there, and I said, 'Hey, do you remember those Stations of the Cross paintings that were in the temporary church?' And he said, 'Oh, yes, I remember those ones, that's right. We threw those away. They weren't any good.' Of course, I wanted them, like in the worst way, yeah. They were very important to me. The colour – you know, black and white and red and all that.

The drama of those panels was absorbed into what seemed, to Scully, a surreal stage on which his life was playing out – a stage he has often described as 'vaudevillian'.

ss All these funny people that I met have made me very colourful. I grew up in a theatrical, travellers' kind of vaudeville. All these figures made me feel that the world was like an artwork. It was a huge artwork. And you know about Vick, of course?

Scully is referring to a cross-dressing comedian who lodged at the house where he lived with his grandmother in Highbury, after his family relocated from the Old Kent Road.

ss Wonderful Vick. We all used the same bathroom. He looked like Samuel Beckett. Vick was Jewish and had beautiful blond hair. He was very tall and had arms like birds' wings. He was gangly, and he would come in and say [whispering], 'Hello kids...' And immediately we'd start laughing. We knew he'd do something funny. He had this trick: he'd pull the door so that it would hit the toe of his shoe and just miss his nose, and then he would fall around. He had this incredible way of falling. He looked like a twig man. It was so wonderful. He was like a performance artist.

Just how deeply into the soil of Scully's imagination these seeds burrowed themselves is impossible to measure: the cerulean bike and the lorry's ladder, the winding barber's pole and the clamour of rain on the tin roof of the makeshift chapel, the vanished panels of the Stations of the Cross and the infectious antics of the cross-dressing comedian with whom Scully shared his childhood. But at some stage, he must have made a conscious decision to pursue art as a profession. What, I wondered, was the catalyst?

ss Well, you know, I've written on the importance of that Picasso painting to me.

Scully is referring to an article that he wrote for the *Irish Examiner* in August 2013, titled 'Effect of the past on the now', in which he describes the formative influence of a reproduction of Picasso's 1901 painting *Child with a Dove* on his emerging imagination. It hung, he says, in the assembly hall of one of his schools, a place 'where we met every day to appreciate our blessings... almost like an altarpiece'. His schooldays still shudder in Scully's memory. 'Next to our school,' he recalled, 'in the compound of the gas works, stood mountains of slag, which is dead coal. Even in death, its dust impregnated itself into all the molecules in the air around us, clinging to our hair and clothes.' Amid the filth, the Picasso reproduction loomed like a promise of salvation. 'I saw it five times a week, for four years,' Scully wrote. 'The composition is utterly simple, and the figure of the child is made by outlining everything in black. This gives it a sacred quality and separates it from its landscape background. In the foreground, falling out of the painting, is a coloured ball that the child must have played with before taking the dove in its hands, as an image of transcendental repose.'

Child with Dove for Oisin, 2013

ss That painting had a profound effect on me. It was a shitty poster. Every day I would see that painting, from eight to eleven. I saw that painting 1,000 times. I think it was transformative. Because it was such a counterweight to all the violence in the school where I was. But then the crucial part comes later, doesn't it? How the hell did I get out of working in a factory in Notting Hill, where my father wilfully put me, to getting into art school and then university? That is still a mystery to me.

To pivot, as Scully did, from a life of menial labour in a printmaking factory in Notting Hill when he was a teenager in the early 1960s to pursuing a career as an esteemed artist less than a decade later is, indeed, nothing short of remarkable. But I was intrigued by Scully's confession that the elements that made such a metamorphosis possible remained to this day 'a mystery' to him. Was there no one in his life who encouraged him or helped to facilitate such a transformation?

ss It was all me. I remember I even went to Forest Hill girls' school [Sydenham School] on Dartmouth Road to do evening classes. I would do anything I could get, like a traveller. Travellers get what they can, and I've always been like that. I've never been one for feeling sorry for myself. As you know, I don't have any self-pity. I just saw all these possibilities. I remember we used to go to a rock 'n' roll café, 'cause I used to be in a gang.

Scully's rough-and-tumble upbringing and involvement in gangs of petty criminals is a recurring theme in our conversations, and a topic to which he returns, registering some surprise, like a butterfly recalling with mild shock the ungainly grub from which it evolved. In a brief reminiscence that Scully wrote in 2004, recalling a childhood friendship, he meditated on the criminal context of his adolescence and its curious parallels with a consciousness of creativity. 'A lot of my young friends were criminals,' he wrote, 'me included... A criminal is an artist without hope. So the dance can't take place and it all goes wrong. You become a vortex of negative energy, the antidote to creativity. There are creative thieves, but it's all in the service of stealing.'

ss This would be around '62. I went to all these rock 'n' roll cafés. They used to have jukeboxes, and you'd have all these Teddy boys coming in, all that sort of business. I remember this guy came up from Devon or somewhere. He was kind of a hippie. And the owner of the café had mysteriously, oddly, commissioned him to paint the Seven Dwarfs on the windows. Snow White and the Seven Dwarfs. This guy had two women with him who looked like Joan Baez, and I remember being fascinated by him. You know, I really admired him. I know that what he was doing wasn't high art, of course, but nevertheless he was an artist. He was living the life of an artist, and I just found it so attractive. He seemed to be much more aware of something 'other'.

KG And he stays in your imagination?

ss Yeah, and I always wanted to find him. He's probably departed by now because he was older. He would have been 20 and I would have been 15, so he would be very old now. Maybe he's down in Devon somewhere making his funny paintings, as people do in Devon. He was very important to me, symbolically. He never noticed me, but I noticed him. Every time I went there, I was looking at him.

KG He just had this aura?

ss Yeah, I kind of hero-worshipped him. And I remember this other time that my life started to get very focused on art, when I fell off a scaffold and nearly got killed. I was working for a plastering company somewhere in Primrose Hill. When I was in this building, I could see down into an apartment: the ground-floor flat of a house that was occupied by a married couple. He was an abstract painter. She used to have breakfast with him and then go off to work. And he'd stay and make these paintings. You could see him painting. I just thought it was so fantastic.

The vision Scully had of an artistic life – one that seemed almost within his physical grasp from the precarious perch of the plasterer's scaffold – could not have revealed itself to him at a more crucial moment. Following a stint as an apprentice typesetter, he found a position working as a graphic designer just off Chancery Lane in central London.

ss   Then it was really revving up, you know. I was going to the Central School of Art to do life drawing at night. I was very dedicated. I was very willing to do all of this alone.

KG   Were you living at home at the time?

ss   Yeah, but my parents didn't have the slightest interest. They thought maybe this was something I'd get over. Of course, to expect somebody to come from life on the run and the slums of Dublin, living with travellers, to go all the way through the strata of society to get where I eventually got – it isn't something you would expect to happen.

Scully is referring, of course, to the full arc of his life's unlikely trajectory. He was born in abject poverty in June 1945 in Dublin, Ireland. His parents had been taken off the streets temporarily and were living in a 7 × 7 ft borrowed basement room in a slum in Inchicore, so that an address could be entered on the baby Sean's birth certificate – a prerequisite of being issued one – before returning to the uncertainties of life in travellers' campsites.

His father would serve time in prison for desertion, an act of conscience that seemed to run in the family. In 1922, John Scully, the artist's 'eponymous grandfather', while awaiting execution for the same offence, had hanged himself to death. After his death, his wife, Scully's grandmother, held on to his name and transferred it to the children she would later have, including the artist's father. Scully's was a family that saw the future as a tentative land – one there was no guarantee of reaching intact. Success, which had always eluded them, would have meant playing by the rules. Painting, whether it was between the lines or the lines themselves, seems to have struck Scully's parents as, at best, an exercise in aloofness and, at worst, improvident insolence in the face of life's callous uncertainties.

ss Of course they were worried. They thought it was reckless and arrogant. It is arrogant! But without all that arrogance, I wouldn't have been able to overcome all the obstacles. And the obstacles were myriad. There was certainly resistance, and a tremendous amount of social discomfort.

KG From friends?

ss My friends couldn't figure out what the hell was wrong with me. I remember once I was talking to this young woman, a girlfriend of one of my friends. I said, 'You know, I could get a lock-up garage. They have lock-up garages where you can actually live and put a bed and make paintings.' I remember she turned around, looked at me and said, 'What's wrong with you?'

When I left my job [at a company called Finnemore & Field to pursue art], there was disapproval and disappointment because I'd broken the apprenticeship. I remember there was a graphic designer at Finnemore & Field called Mr Russell, who was sort of an old communist and loved Picasso. When I said I wanted to go to art school, he said

Blanket Hung Above Chair, 1964
Two Figures, Interior Scene, 1964

Cactus, 1964

to somebody, 'Well, if he doesn't get in, it won't matter.' He didn't think much of me, in other words, and he wasn't the only one. Nobody did. I got turned down by all the art schools. All of them.

KG Well, save one.

The 'one' was Croydon School of Art, where Scully was enrolled between 1965 and 1968. It was here that he would first become interested in Van Gogh, as well as Emil Nolde, Karl Schmidt-Rottluff and Henri Matisse – antecedents who would indelibly mark the aspiring artist's imagination. Crucially, it was at Croydon that Scully would find himself obsessed with the liberating lexicon of abstract expressionism.

SS Every single art school turned me down, except the art school for true oddballs – Croydon – which is where John Rocha, Malcolm McLaren and Ray Davies went.

KG What did the application to these schools entail? What was being rejected when you were being rejected?

SS My work, I suppose. I had that fabulous little cactus painting, which is a beautiful little painting. Even now, people admire it. But even that couldn't get me in. I don't know what it was. I must have had about me the ambience of a kind of apprentice gangster. All these obstacles that were put in my way, I just wouldn't accept defeat.

For many people, such seamless, serial rejection would have been soul-crushing. Scully's perseverance paid off, and when he finally arrived at Croydon School of Art he knew a new world had opened up to him. Things would never be the same again.

Gray Zig Zag, 1970

A Bedroom in Venice

ss When I finally got into art school, I thought that heaven had fallen down and embraced me. I can't tell you what it meant to me. It's indescribable, beyond measure. I had the opportunity to be an artist. It was my dream.

That 'dream' had been sculpted somewhat by the reality of what was possible. The doors that had finally opened for Scully were not necessarily the ones through which every aspiring art student fantasized about skipping. 'I went to a school for idiots,' Scully told an interviewer in 2014, 'because I got turned down by every other art school. I didn't have much visible talent. So I got into Croydon School of Art, and I found that I had a very strong intellectual structure, somehow; I had a tenacious intellect.' What Croydon lacked in prestige, however, it made up for in kindness and encouragement. It was the right place at the right time, and precisely the environment Scully needed in order to grow as an artist.

ss I'm deeply grateful to England for that, and I always will be. I'm very appreciative of England and all the people that helped me, too. And the teachers that were there. Barry Hirst – my God, he had an enormous effect on me.

Scully's affection for his early mentor is itself very affecting. A whole history is waiting to be written on the fundamental role of attentive and inspiring teachers in the shaping of art history, from Leonardo's apprenticeship under Andrea del Verrocchio in 15th-century Florence to Thomas Hart Benton's intense and intriguingly sublimated tuition of Jackson Pollock in America in

Bend 1, 1968

Square, 1969

the 20th century. What is it, exactly, that Scully so fondly recalls of his early instructor's teaching?

ss His belief in me, and opening all the doors on how to paint and use colour. He would use sound and say, 'Find a colour that makes that sound.' One thing he said to me that I've always stuck by: 'Always use the biggest brush you can.' Isn't that interesting? So, in other words, don't be petty. Don't be small. Be big. Brushstroke never lies. Brushstroke is the fingerprint of your soul. Your whole personality will register in the way that you swing the brush.

Scully, of course, would spend years, especially in the 1970s, ploughing a minimalist furrow with a relatively narrow brush, before finally embracing the big, broad handyman bristles for which he has become famous. So did Hirst's advice just crouch in his mind like a ticking time bomb?

ss It did. And this was given to me by Barry Hirst, who is a massive figure for me. Later, I suffered an incredible crisis in New York. I knew in my heart that minimalism would not continue to develop because it was based on reduction. Anything that's based on reduction cannot provide raw material going forward because you're basically refining it. If we take, for example, the metaphor of sugar, refined sugar is no good. It's not good for you. It doesn't support human life. I noticed that all the people that were involved in minimalism were somehow aristocratic. They weren't of the world. They weren't of the street. They weren't like blues singers. They weren't from a working-class, brute state. They weren't rough. None of that was allowed. It was all refined out. I thought, 'I have to break it.' And then, of course, I made my famous painting *Backs and Fronts*.

In 1981, Scully had a breakthrough. After years of pushing, as far as he could, the possibilities of minimalist abstraction, as pioneered

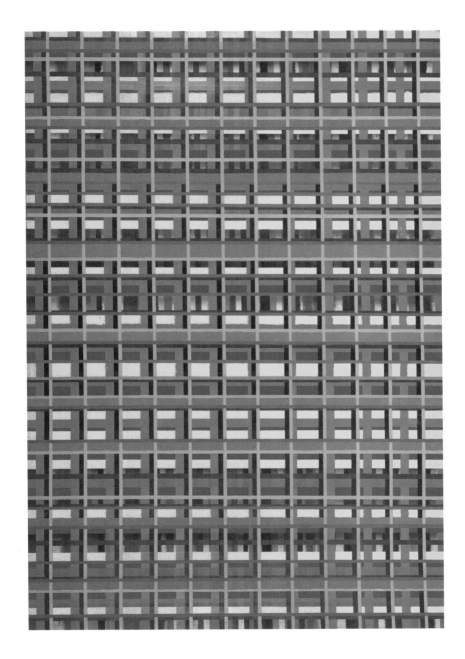

Bridge, 1970

Backs and Fronts, 1981

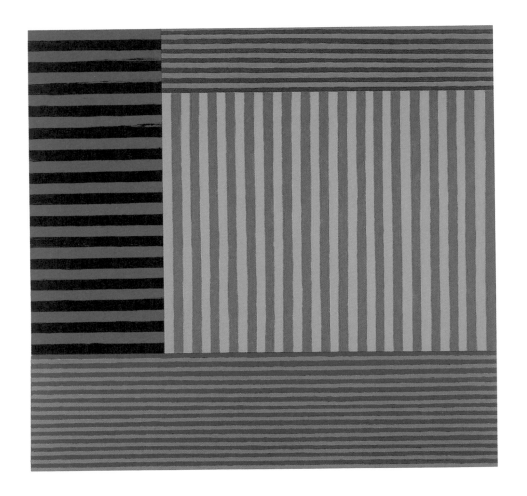

Blue, 1981

in the late 1950s by Frank Stella and championed throughout the 1960s and 1970s by such artists as Carl Andre and Donald Judd, he rejected the genre's relentless eschewal of human emotion. Having come to believe that minimalism had turned its back on people – on the intimacies and urgencies of what it means to be alive in the world – by erasing from its surface all traces of life's roughness, Scully set about saving painting and rescuing abstraction by restoring a human energy to its simple geometries. His work of the 1970s had been characterized by immaculate measurements and miles of masking tape that had helped to ensure the artist never painted outside the lines and stayed true to the careful calibrations of minimalism's austerities. His 1981 manifesto painting *Backs and Fronts* changed all that. Its colossal size and conjoined panels of varying widths and heights rejected the most fundamental premise on which painting rested: the rectangle. The work's ragged top and bottom edges, which soared and plummeted like a jagged skyline crammed with skyscrapers, was invested with added edginess by a rough, gestural freedom that varied from panel to panel. To achieve such dynamism and expression, the tight bristles of surgically slender 'minimalist' brushes had to go.

ss The way I got to all that was, as you say, a ticking time bomb. I thought, 'How did I paint when I was with Barry? How did I paint when he would come and see me every couple of days?' I just combined how I was painting then with how I was painting later, and came up with my breakthrough paintings.

In retrospect, the breakthrough that Scully is describing – which manifested itself not only in *Backs and Fronts*, but in a host of other paintings created around this time, including *Araby*, *Enough*, *Blue* and *Precious* (works – all dating from 1981 – whose creation he and I would go on to discuss in greater depth later in our conversations) – proved crucial to the unfolding narrative of abstract art in the last quarter of the 20th century. But that breakthrough was not instrumental in establishing Scully as a formidable force in geometric painting in the 1970s and early 1980s. If anything, challenging the orthodoxy of minimalism was risky to his prospects and reputation. Though minimalism was flawed, it was nevertheless the dominant movement. It, and its adherents, were in control in New York, where Scully was living from the mid-1970s, having abandoned Britain. Had he decided to continue driving in the same lane and not rocked the boat (to muddle my metaphors), he could comfortably have maintained a position as a leading light in minimalism alongside Stella, Andre and Judd.

Scully's instinct to shift course, though risky and unnecessary from a commercial perspective at the time, doubtless resulted in his being a far more significant figure in the story of art. It wasn't the first time he had followed his gut. At an even earlier stage, after being accepted into the art school in Newcastle University in 1968, he was faced with a more fundamental decision: what kind of painter would he be? Would he continue to paint figuratively recognizable objects of this world, such as the cactus still life that won him a place at Croydon, and the seated figures of 1967 that smudged reality into a Fauvist puzzle of substance and shadow? Or would he devote himself instead to exploring a more thoroughgoing language of uncompromising abstraction? We know, of course, the direction he chose. But I was keen to ask him, with the benefit of hindsight, how he perceived that crossroads more than half a century later?

ss In the movie *The Charge of the Light Brigade*, after a catastrophic charge through the Khyber Pass, the Sergeant says, 'Go again, sir!' which is not something I would have said. But with life I would certainly say, 'Can I have another go?' And if I had another go, then I would have played it out as a figurative painter.

KG Really?

Madonna, 2019

ss Well, I could have done either, and figuration has made a huge comeback, as has abstraction. They're both fascinating to me. Of course, I did play out figuration with 'Eleuthera'.

By 'Eleuthera', Scully is referring to a series of paintings collectively named after an island in the Bahamian archipelago. These figurative works in oil on aluminium, begun in 2015, are based on photographs the artist took of his son, Oisin, kneeling on the beach and playing in the sand. In each, the boy is encircled by a protective, if fragile, moat that has been scooped out around him. In an offshoot series created in 2018 and 2019, entitled 'Madonna', Oisin is joined in the tender enclosure by the loving presence of his mother, Liliane Tomasko, the artist's wife. The two series – 'Eleuthera' and 'Madonna' – mark Scully's return to figurative painting after having abandoned the tradition in art school. The artist's re-engagement with representational painting is remarkably seamless. The composition of these recent works is uncannily in accord with experiments from half a century earlier. Puzzled together from large fragments of ripe colour like a toddler's first jigsaw, 'Eleuthera' and 'Madonna' both attest to the brittleness of the ties that bind us – how quickly connections can be shattered into a meaningless jumble, or simply washed away by a breaking wave. Placed alongside Scully's acres of abstract lines and blocks, the figurative works feel surprisingly at peace and of a piece, as if the line between the two genres had always been more fluid than we acknowledge or admit – a difference in degree rather than kind.

ss I suppose I thought that abstraction was somehow more of our time, that it was connected to structures that we would need in the future, and that we would need these ways of thinking about how we organize structures. I wanted to be involved in that, but at the same time I didn't want us to forget where we came from. The fact that we have bodies and we sit around the campfire, and we like to climb trees.

For that, of course, you need to have trees. I didn't want to forget all that. So that's why I included this insistence on the brushstroke. I think it was a painful decision for me in a certain way.

I always think of popular music as music with words. I liken that to figuration. I always think of abstract painting as more high-minded but more rarefied and, to some degree, isolated. Certainly in England, abstraction is not understood nearly as well as figuration. So if I'd continued with figuration (and I was hugely admired for those figurative paintings), I would have become like my friend David Hockney. You know, David says that a figurative painting will always be more valuable than an abstract painting, and he might be right. An abstract painting can get monotonous, as somebody once wrote about my work. I agree: it can get monotonous. You have to struggle with that. It's very high-minded.

KG Were you drawn to the crisis?

SS The project I set myself could be described in a couple of ways. One is: how to popularize abstract painting. Or how to pull together all its strands of potential into one work, or one body of work. And that's kind of the project I set myself.

KG Was that conscious, at the time – the project of making abstract painting more popular?

SS How am I going to realize, manifest, all its potential, which hasn't been pulled together? Of course, abstract painting has found great popularity with, for example, Mondrian and Rothko, let's say. I've taken a lot from both of them, but particularly Mondrian, because what I took from Rothko already existed in Romantic painting in Europe – in Turner, for example. I took a lot from Mondrian – his ideas of rhythm.

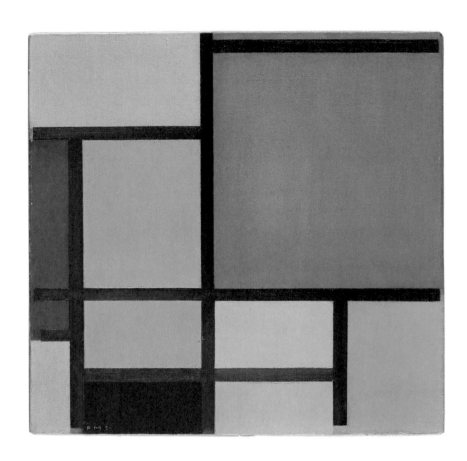

Piet Mondrian, *Composition*, 1921

But I tried to make them more of the street, you know, more knockabout, so that people could get into them. Because I find Mondrian rather exclusionary.

KG His works are pristine, aren't they? There's little of the mess of life.

SS That's what I don't like about them. I mean, it's what I admire about them, and what I don't like about them.

Scully's indebtedness to Mondrian is a subject the artist himself has taken some pains to trace and explain. 'What I loved about Mondrian', he observed in 1995, in notes compiled for a prospective lecture, 'was the timeless and "repressed" emotion in his work. In my own work I think this ethic of having the emotion somehow embedded within the structure (rather than obviously expressed through overt gesture or subject matter) is crucially important. This connects Mondrian to the great pantheon of classical artists that we have produced in Europe. For me, I think this comes from a sense of morality, a sense that somehow an art work should be profound and timeless.'

SS You know Mondrian went to Ben Nicholson's studio, which is just down the road from our new house in Hampstead.

KG Yeah, it's literally a stone's throw.

SS Yeah. Ben Nicholson said, 'What do you think [of the place]?' and Mondrian replied, 'Too much nature.' Well, I think personally you can't get enough nature and we don't have enough nature. But, of course, our needs have changed. Our relationship to nature has changed. The existential threat that we face was not apparent to Mondrian, who was hell-bent on getting rid of nature, even though he started out as a tree painter.

KG Well, he was looking for the essence, or spirit of nature, stripped of impurity.

SS Yeah. We've realized now, to our regret, that's actually dangerous – to take the world on that kind of mental path. It removes us from what we are now desperately trying to restore, having, you know, pulverized it for centuries. And my work is, of course, an embrace of that; my work is not abstract in the same way at all, and I don't want it to be. I make it metaphorical and, in a way, figurative.

KG In your mind, the line between abstraction and figuration isn't so clear – the two blur into one. In a sense, your line is a body; your line is a figure. It isn't opposed to figuration: it subsumes figuration.

SS That is the crux of the problem that I faced, certainly in New York where people had a lot of trouble trying to figure out what I was doing.

KG I suppose, for them, the minimalist line really was a complete rejection of all things human.

SS Yeah, and I found it, at its worst, to have aspects of fascism about it. Because if you look at all the visual paraphernalia of fascism, it's always clean. It's always geometric, usually with primary, unnuanced colours. Because nuance is dangerous for fascism. Nuance pollutes the clarity of fascism. And this is one of the reasons why I do what I do, and why I feel very strongly about it. I see this as political, and I see fascism as a constant danger.

KG And were there fascist elements at play in how minimalism asserted its dominance as an aesthetic movement when you moved to New York in the 1970s?

ss Very much so, by a handful of players who had full control over the mechanisms of power. There were two competing forces, to put it simply – of course it's an oversimplification. There was the Greenbergian force [Clement Greenberg, who dismissed minimalism as a novelty] and then there were the minimalists themselves, and they were at loggerheads. The minimalists finally won because they had the support of Europe. It was very tightly strung and precious. And prescribed – the language was prescribed.

I remember once, my friend Per Jensen and I were invited, second-hand, to a party of Barbara Haskell's. Barbara Haskell is an old-time curator at the Whitney who made a show of Agnes Martin, whom I love. Bob [Robert] Ryman said we could go. Bob was very kind to me. He was an angelic person. He's just about the nicest person I've ever met in the art world. We went to the party, but Bob, it turned out, couldn't come. So Per and I went, and there we were, these young skinny boys at this party. It was so snooty, it was incredible. I remember there was a guy asking us what we were doing there. It was extremely exclusionary, very refined. It was as if we were being allowed (or not) into a Shinto shrine, and in the end we were considered to be too grubby, so they threw us out. That's how inhospitable New York was – you know, without any sense of kindness or hospitality at all.

KG This is around what year? The mid- to late 1970s?

ss Yeah, about '77.

KG By then you were fully resident in New York.

ss Oh yeah, and I was making paintings that a lot of people thought were interesting. I have to say, I was pretty shocked by it. But now, of course, I find it pretty funny.

I find it very difficult to maintain grudges. I always let things go, you know? Because I have this explosive temperament. My son loves it and says to me, 'Daddy, you're very rough, but when it's over, it's over!' You know, my parents used to hold on to things and it gave me a terrible stomach ache.

I was in the Museum of Modern Art and I bumped into my old friend Aggie [Agnes] Gund, who is a wonderful woman, a friend to artists, and a huge supporter of the museum. I'd had an operation on my shoulder and my arm was in a sling, so she asked me what had happened. Simultaneously, she introduced me to a woman who was a video artist. Well, being slightly provocative and impish as I am, when she asked me what happened, I said, 'I fell off a ladder in my studio.' And then, to enlarge this drama, I said I was wounded in the service of art. It had exactly the desired result. It was almost as automatic as flipping a light switch. This woman, the video artist, became incredibly inflamed and said [screeching], 'Well, you shouldn't make such big paintings then, should you!' And there it was, unpacked: years of nurturing resentment.

The Museum of Modern Art (MoMA) is the setting for any number of stories in Scully's colourful repertoire – vignettes that shed light on how he felt he was received by the art world. Scully went on to tell me how 'incredibly important' Gund herself had been to him, what 'a great ally' she had been. He fondly recalled her generous donation to the museum of a fabulous painting of his from 1988, *A Bedroom in Venice*, whose surface seems to absorb into tranquil rhythms of brushed blues – one minute pale and wistful, the next rich and dusky – so many of those archetypal elements that implanted themselves in his imagination in childhood: the cerulean of his tricycle, the red and white stripes of the barber's pole he would pedal past in his neighbourhood on the Old Kent Road, and even, in the mirroring inset on the left

CHAPTER TWO

A Bedroom in Venice, 1988

No Neo, 1984

in the painting, a semblance of the rungs of that lorry's ladder that he daydreamed might lift him to a mystical elsewhere. Reminiscing about MoMA soon brought back to Scully another encounter and a more complicated shade of blue.

ss   We went to MoMA once with my parents.

By 'we', Scully means he and his then-wife Catherine Lee, the painter.

ss   My parents were very self-obsessed, and my brother used to refer to us – making a riff on the army surplus stores that had opened up and proliferated all over London after the war, when they had all that army surplus shit to get rid of – as 'surplus to requirements'. It's a nice phrase, isn't it? My parents used to sit in the kitchen, in this very narrow room with a little pink Formica table that we christened 'pretty'. And they would be at each end, jammed up against the wall. My brother and I would be on the long side, and we had to sit in silence while they just talked about work. My mother would have a kind of therapy session with my father. She would talk about all the enemies she'd made at work and who'd said what, who shouldn't have said this, who shouldn't have said that, who told him not to, and who will tell him not to in the future – that sort of thing.
      Anyway, we went to MoMA because my parents came to New York to visit. By an extraordinary coincidence, a painting of mine was hanging near the entrance, a painting called *No Neo*, which is one of my favourite paintings. I love the title because it was against neo-geo [neo-geometric conceptualism]. Because there was neo-expressionism and then neo-geo, by the time neo-geo came around I'd had more than enough 'neo'. So anyway, we go into the museum and there I am with Catherine and my parents, and there is a painting hanging by their son in the temple of modern art – the

greatest collection of modern art in the world. So they stop and they look. I said, 'Wow, I didn't know that was hanging', because MoMA were considering buying it. But they didn't buy it because they were too short-sighted. My mother rather astutely said to me, 'That blue on the painting is a blue that you don't use very often.' I was amazed that she knew that. I always assumed they'd paid scant attention to my work, to my career, because they found it so bizarre. And then I said to my mother, 'Yes, you know, you're absolutely right. I didn't think of it myself, but you're right.' I very rarely use that kind of blue, which in a sense goes back a little bit to cerulean – it wasn't really cerulean blue, but it was brilliant. And then my father's contribution was – and this is a perfect quote – 'Well, that's enough of that.'

Scully and I laugh, but I am aware that this is more than just an amusing anecdote. It reveals an awareness he had of the difference between his mother's attention and attentiveness and that of his father. Or was it possible the dismissive comment 'that's enough of that' concealed a deeper interest or understanding that, perhaps, his father was too embarrassed to confess? I wondered, was there ever a moment when Scully and his father discussed what it was he had been trying to accomplish through his art? I had barely posed the question when Scully's side split with almost uncontrollable laughter at the suggestion.

ss   The answer is no! I will recount to you one story that happened early on. He had a guy in Hatton Garden jewelry market...

Scully is referring to one of his father's regular customers. When Scully was very young, still living on the Old Kent Road, his father worked in a barbershop that was just down the street. He would eventually move to a more prestigious location and clientele in Holborn, around the corner from Hatton Garden. To say that Scully's relationship with his father was complicated would be a serious understatement. There are countless anecdotes of heart-wrenching tension between the two, as well as recollections of real affection, often conveyed in a language that goes out of its way to discern, in retrospect, a common ground that eluded them at the time – an affinity that lay deeper than the surface frictions that seemed to characterize their relationship. 'He had beautiful hands,' Scully told the art curator and critic Hans Ulrich Obrist in an interview, 'and he thought of himself as an artist. He entered the Barber of Britain contest, and he came fourth. He was the fourth most proficient barber in Britain.'

ss This was around the time I first went to art school. My father came home and he was smiling like a cat, you know in the way that a cat would smile after it had caught something. He said, 'Well, I've got £5 for you.' In those days, that was quite a sum of money. He said that his customer, whom I knew – a pleasant man who went fishing at the weekends – wanted me to paint a picture of him in his fishing boat. I said, 'Um, I don't think I can do that.' This happened after I'd committed myself, at least temporarily, to the pursuit of abstraction – which took over my energy and all my psychology, of course. My father had got himself into this difficult situation, and the client's view of him was significantly more important than my view of him. That was always clear. In the order of things, we were, as my brother said, surplus to requirements. Except on this occasion I had something, or my dad had something, that he could then parlay to gain prestige with his client, and that was a son who was an artist. Of course, he would brag about this in the barbershop, which was a big barbershop. It had thirteen chairs. And he'd commissioned me without my consent to make this painting. I said, 'I can't do it.' He became extremely agitated and angry and said, 'You mean, you're unable to do it, or you don't have the talent to do it?' Because people thought that art was all about talent. I replied, 'No, I do have the talent, physically, to do it, but I can't do it because I'm involved in something else that's taking all my energy.' Then he said, having cornered me on the chessboard of life, 'You mean you won't do it?' To cut a long story short, and to truncate any more misunderstandings, I said, 'That's right. I won't do it.'

Wow! All I can say is that we experienced in that little kitchen a mini-Ice Age that went on for a very long time. Because my father used silence as a weapon against us, as a prelude to possible violence. Neither of my parents were that groovy, you know. One gave you a headache, and the other gave you a stomach ache. It was tremendously stressful. So, you see, when I went to New York, I was quite ready. Nobody can give me the cold shoulder because I grew up with the cold shoulder. I'm cold-shoulder-proof.

KG The cold shoulder was the warm glow you grew up in.

SS Yeah.

KG How long did the Ice Age last?

SS Oh, they would take, at a minimum, a week. And everybody would suffer.

Scully went on to share with me, as he has many times before, other incidents of intense tension between him and his father. As he did so, I couldn't help wondering to what extent the very spirit of the work he would go on to create, which he has often described as stemming from a desire to find order in disorder, harmony in discord, owed something to these terrible skirmishes.

KG You know, in the past I've always understood the conflict and frictions in your work in archetypal terms – darkness versus light, or evil versus good – but is there a more intimate level, a more urgent one, on which your paintings function? Were you driven by a desire to find harmony or to choreograph the chaos that was your home?

ss Yeah. The wonderful writer who wrote that piece on me in the *Financial Times* said that my paintings are alter egos.

Scully is alluding to an article by the art critic Rachel Spence that appeared in the *FT* in September 2018, on the occasion of an important display of his work at the Yorkshire Sculpture Park in England, as well as a major exhibition at the Smithsonian Institution's Hirshhorn Museum in Washington, DC. In her eloquent piece, Spence manages to capture beautifully the complex relationship – at once physical and psychological – between creator and created. 'Scully is a big man,' Spence observes. 'Although he walks a little stiffly due to a bad back, he has the broad shoulders and long limbs of an athlete. His voice, still rooted in his London childhood, regularly booms off the pale walls in full-caps outrage. Whether he is discussing Donald Trump ("a collective insanity") or his own journey ("my story is like Lazarus but I didn't die"), I am left in no doubt that his paintings' apparent serenity makes them the alter ego of a troubled soul.'

ss In a certain sense I think I might have given up on order. But I still use systems, or approaches, that have a lot to do with stacking – which, I guess, has to do with order, doesn't it? Recently, with 'Black Square', I've entirely given up on trying to make things fit. Or what I'm saying is that things don't fit.

'Black Square' refers to a series of works that Scully embarked on during lockdown, at the height of the COVID-19 pandemic in 2020. His otherwise busy calendar of exhibition openings at venues around the globe was scrubbed when the world ground to a halt. Isolating in New York with his wife, the artist Liliane

Black Square, 2020

Tomasko, and his 10-year-old son, Oisin, Scully seized the opportunity to respond directly to the anguish of the unfolding crisis. The 'Black Square' series, painted in oil on aluminium, converses directly with the Russian artist Kazimir Malevich's famous painting of the same name (1915), reimagining that monochromatic milestone a century earlier as an invasive virus that inserts itself in the imagination and replicates. In Scully's vision, *Black Square* is a haunting painting-within-a-painting – a work suspended in an ether of broad, thickly applied horizontal stripes of weary but resilient colour that only Scully could have painted. When an early iteration of Scully's *Black Square* was posted on social media, it caused something of a stir. Capturing at once the sense of isolation the world was feeling, it was also strangely uplifting – the bands of colour becoming rippling waves of hope, fortitude and resolve that keep despair in check and stop it from overwhelming the bigger picture.

KG There's an abyss deepening at the heart of it.

SS Yeah. I wonder why it's taken so long to get to it. It took this existential epidemic that we have to push me over the line.

Untitled (Newcastle #1), 1969

CHAPTER THREE

Newcastle Boogie-Woogie

ss   What has really surprised me, beguiled me, is the extraordinary return of painting, which everybody had written off
when I was a young artist. People would say things like, 'At
least I'm not painting.' They would say, 'How are you doing?'
and you'd say, 'I am doing great: I'm not painting.' The
absence of painting was, in itself, a value. Isn't it amazing
how the world has changed?

KG   When you were at art school in Newcastle, you experimented
with sculpture. Did you ever think, 'Maybe painting hasn't
got a lot of legs left in it, perhaps I should put my shoulder
into sculpture instead'? Or were you always fully committed?

ss   Well, the thing about me is this: I never drive by a wounded
animal. That's deep inside me. I don't want to make too
much of the psychology of this, but I did have the animal
hospital at 58 Tannsfeld Road [in Sydenham], which I have
written about.

When Scully was twelve, his family settled in 'sunny Sydenham',
south London, where he soon set up a makeshift veterinary clinic
in the 'small conservatory at the back of their small house'. The
house, he recalled in a short prose sketch from 2001, was 'of
the terraced, claustrophobic variety, with pebbledash walls and
bay windows... When I pass it now, it doesn't look anything like
a freelance animal hospital run by an under-age doctor!... Most
of the cases were hopeless, and that didn't change; but a few
of them were not, and that didn't change either.' There, Scully
put into practice the healing techniques he had learned from a

neighbour, an elderly lady with whom he would spend time when he wasn't 'busy painting and breaking into people's houses': 'We met across a great divide of time and knowledge (plenty on her side, and none on mine) over the issue of animals – their wonderful nervous world, the relationship between their little lives and their little deaths… I would take in [a] sparrow, feed it a little crushed aspirin. I'd put the bird at the end of a woollen sock and then hang [the sock] on [a] nail in the room, black and quiet under the stairs, just like she [had] showed me. The next day I would take it out, fix its wing, and feed it. I felt as if I was connected to everything. Later on, when I became a painter, I tried to fill my paintings with love and with this refusal to give up that I learned from the wounded animals, that I learned through her.'

ss I think that's a major part of my nature.

I found the connection between making art and caring for wounded creatures fascinating, and asked Scully whether he had consciously made that link himself when he set out to be an artist.

ss Oh, absolutely. That's why I identified so much with Vincent van Gogh, because he tried to make the world a better place – you know, as Don McLean sings in 'Vincent', 'This world was never meant for one / As beautiful as you.' It's an absolutely heartbreaking song, especially the way McLean sings it – with that clear, night-sky voice. I always equated art with reform, with betterment, with healing. I never thought of it as something that's just nice to look at. I wouldn't have been one of those artists that wanted to be in the court. I guess I would have been more like Tintoretto than Titian, 'cause Titian had the court all wrapped up, and that left the cold, damp churches to Tintoretto, who's a much crazier painter. And I guess I would have been more like that because I would never have wanted to be in the court; I don't want that kind of acceptance. I always like to be a little bit

Vincent, 2002

'out' – and I am a little bit out, so I am what I desire. I think of art as something profound – as our salvation – because we've done our best to smash the world up in the name of religion. We've devalued and debased religion as much as we can. Of course, it still survives. There's still a spiritual aura that we gravitate to, and I gravitate to it as well. But I always thought of art as something very powerful, very important.

I was never interested in making decorations or having rich people buy my work. And that's interesting in relation to my ultimate rejection of minimalism because, at the time, art was extremely rarefied and elitist. It was supported by only a handful of people. I had a very small audience. What I admire about minimalism, of course, was its severity, because that corresponds with my own sense of moral rigour, my own ethical standards. So minimalism appealed to me. But I didn't like that it was basically supported by people who were aristocratic. They all seemed to be aristocratic in some way. They'd have these giant spaces that cost an arm and a leg, and then they'd have a painting the size of a book hanging on the wall. I just wanted to mess all that up.

KG Who were your early collectors and supporters? Do you remember the first time you sold a work?

SS My very first supporter was Ian Bennett, who was a great man about town. He worked for Sotheby's on Bond Street and he was a real dandy who knew everybody, like a 20th-century Beau Brummell – a guy who got by on his charm. He came to Newcastle and I'd made the painting *Blaze*, which really blew everybody's mind up there. In a way, it looked a little bit like an acid painting, and I had dropped acid a few times of course. He walked into my studio with a model who was wearing hot pants, because, you know, he'd go out with all these fashion models. And there they were in a studio in Newcastle, at the other end of the country. It was just so crazy.

'Ian and I became profound friends,' Scully wrote in a eulogy of Bennett, who passed away in 2014. 'When I stayed at his place on my trips over to London from New York, the sound of his primitive typewriter would shake me out of bed as he wrote deep into the night... He was, quite simply, the most informed and intelligent person I had ever met. Yet he was no dry stick. Ian had style. Ian had panache. If he wore a suit, it said something about Mayfair, and if he wore a tie it announced him from across the street. In his pomp, he strolled around Bond Street as if he were its cultural king – a king equipped with urbane wit and cool style.'

ss Ian walked into my studio and said, 'That's great. How much is it?' It's a beautiful story, this. I didn't know what to say. I was so embarrassed that I'd never sold anything – well, I'd sold a couple of figurative paintings at Croydon. I didn't want to say £100 because that seemed excessive, so I said £90. He agreed immediately and just wrote me a cheque. And here's the very beautiful part of the story. Ian lived on Chepstow Road in Notting Hill, in an upstairs apartment, and had the painting sent down from Newcastle. But when it arrived, it didn't fit in his apartment, so he got a different apartment to accommodate a painting that cost the same as the sofa. That, to me, demonstrated his huge love for the painting. He became an incredible supporter of mine.

KG Did he help you get your first gallery?

ss Yeah.

'I strolled around with him,' Scully recalled in his tribute, and 'he mounted a campaign to get me into the Rowan Gallery, which in 1972 was the best gallery in London. With his close friend Jamie Dugdale by his side he succeeded, and I went from art student to art star in the twinkle of an eye.'

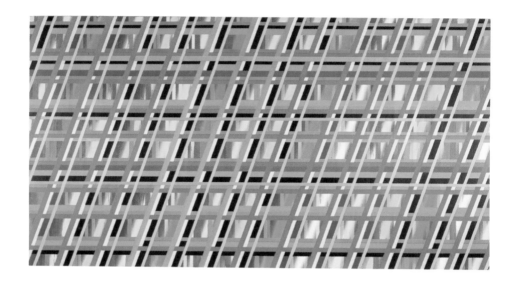

Blaze, 1971

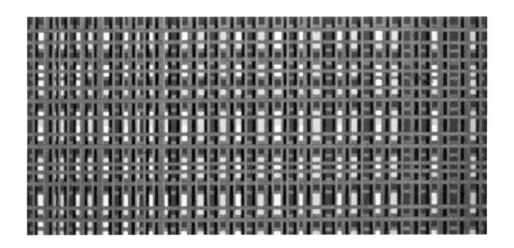

Newcastle Boogie-Woogie, 1971

KG Your first show there was in 1973. What was it like?

SS It was an extraordinary event. I made these 'supergrid' paintings that really stunned everybody. Sure, there had been grids before, but they hadn't been piled up the way I did it, which was influenced by the Wall of Sound. I just layered them over and over again. What I was trying to do, in a sense, was destroy order with order, using it against itself. One sold to the Whitworth [Manchester, UK], one to Belfast [Ulster Museum], one to Cork, one to Sydney, Australia, and one to Melbourne. As well as the five paintings that went to museums, one sold to David Frost, the TV personality, and another to a guy who ran the Impressionist Department at Sotheby's, because Ian worked at Sotheby's. So they were all sold to extremely high-level people, and those paintings are still in those museums.

KG That's not your average first outing for a graduate of art school.

SS No, I was extremely fortunate. It was like a fairy tale. I remember one night before that first show I went round to the gallery to stretch up one of the 'East Coast Light' paintings. I had made these 'East Coast Light' paintings while studying on a fellowship at Harvard earlier that year, as a homage to the Charles River – again, another water type.

Born on the last day of June, Scully is the star sign Cancer, which, in the currency of the zodiac, is the cardinal sign of the water trigon (comprising Cancer, Scorpio and Pisces) – a fact that he believes helpfully describes his fluid nature. 'I am like water,' he has told me. 'If something's in the way, I just go around it... I don't need it to move aside. It doesn't have to.'

SS You know, my mother's signature song was 'Unchained Melody'.

Our chat is free-flowing now, a stream of consciousness, and the mere mention of water brings to Scully's mind the lyrics of the Righteous Brothers' famous song, which his mother used to sing in competitions. He breaks into song about the flow of lonesome rivers. 'My mother was a singer,' Scully wrote in a prose sketch entitled 'Music' in 2014. 'She used to sing on stage. She was almost famous. Her favourite song was "Unchained Melody". Another song, in the river of songs that use the metaphor of flowing water to show that all that we love floats away. Though, it also floats back, in return.'

I chime in by reminding Scully of a story he once told me about an unchecked flow of water in a makeshift studio he occupied in the early 1970s on Tooley Street, near London Bridge, where many of the paintings that would fill his first exhibition at the Rowan Gallery were made. A leak had caused significant damage to the ceiling and had opened up a huge gaping hole in his floor, around which he had to tread carefully for fear of falling in. Poor but promising, Scully was struggling to make ends meet and the aching hole was as much existential as it was architectural.

ss It was hysterically funny. I got the key to a loft, which was in a building owned by British Rail that has now been gentrified, and there was this drip from the roof. Again, it just shows you the power of water. Water brooks no resistance. It was dripping onto the floor, and the floor had the most beautiful hole in it – about 20 ft in diameter. It went through every floor in the building. Drip, drip, drip. Water is an unbelievably powerful force. It was just a drip from a pipe or something, and it went straight down into the basement, which was full of electricity and about 3 ft of water. If you went into the basement, you wouldn't exit! The ceiling was about 8 ft 4 in high, so I had 2 inches at the top and 2 at the bottom of the painting clear. I put a fluorescent strip up because otherwise it would have been impossible for me to view the painting. I had to go outside to look at the colours.

Scully's comments have fluidly slipped into a discussion of one of the paintings he created in the space – one to which he alluded earlier when he mentioned having sold a work from his first commercial show to the Ulster Museum. The painting was initially christened *Fourth Layer* and was later expanded to a slightly longer title that tied it explicitly to its dilapidated origins. *Fourth Layer – Tooley Street* (1973) is among my favourite of Scully's early works, and one that I lingered over in a review of a major retrospective of the artist's career with which the Ulster Museum reopened its doors in 2009, after a huge refurbishment. The painting, so I wrote for the *Times Literary Supplement*, 'manages to create an Escher-like illusion of infinite depth – a sleight of hand that conceals the artist's actual poverty in a mesh of masking tape and optical theories. Only the title locates the painting in the real world, where a leak somewhere in the ceilings above Scully's studio opened a gaping hole that eventually penetrated through his floor. Looked at one way', I concluded, 'the interlocking lines symbolize Scully's attempt to stem the seepage – by braiding the angularity of American Minimalism and the cold mathematics of Op Art into something softer: a safety-net, a gauze for the soul.'

ss Fortunately there were a lot of chairs around, so I circled the hole in the floor with chairs. It would have made a beautiful sculpture. Well, it was a beautiful sculpture! It's a sculpture in my memory now. If I stood back too far, I'd hit the back of a chair and stop before I fell down the hole. The problem with the hole was that the wood wasn't cut. The wood was bent down. It had been persuaded to give way after many years of water just tapping away at it. The building had been abandoned for ten, maybe fifteen years, with this leak in it. The view down to the basement was also very beautiful. Of course, it was a bit hairy to look down, you know.

I have a very weak sense of danger. I also say things sometimes and wonder if I should have said it. I say things that

Fourth Layer – Tooley Street, 1973

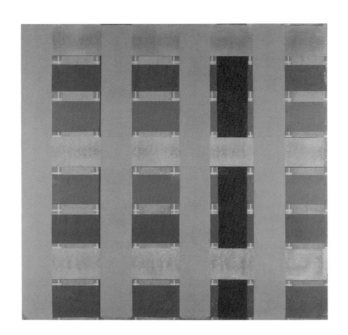

Crossover Painting #1, 1974
Taped Painting Cream and Black, 1975

are not filtered. Of course, that reveals a lot of truth too. You can't have it both ways. You can't be a politician and an artist at the same time. I've got a wonderful story to tell you about Berkeley Square as a counterweight to this.

We've now come full circle, picking up from where we left off, before we took a detour into the depths of water in Scully's imagination and work. Scully is returning to the 'fairy tale' of his landing heavyweight representation at the highly sought-after Rowan Gallery – which at the time was located just off Berkeley Square, on Bruton Place – while still in his mid-twenties, and a comical episode that took place on its premises when he had been left there unsupervised one evening. Circling back to an unfinished topic in this way is something Scully does with rhetorical ease, as if by design, and one senses that he is aware of the larger shape of a conversation – how its blocks and lines fit together to create an organic whole.

ss   There I am in this studio that is about as edgy and dangerous as you can get. The only thing that would make it more dangerous would be a gunfight. As a counterbalance to this, I had to put *East Coast Light 2* back on its stretcher. So I went round to the Rowan Gallery to stretch it out. I cannot tell you how beautiful Alex Gregory-Hood [the founder of the gallery] was. He kind of ruined me because he was so adorable. When he finally retired and then died, it was kind of impossible for me to love anybody else. In a way, my career got off to such a wonderful start that it was a disaster for subsequent relationships. Alex was minor aristocracy, allegedly related to Robin Hood, and he lived at Loxley Hall [in Warwickshire]. There you had a contrast of opposites: you had this boy from the underclass being taken on by an extremely privileged man who was running this gallery right around the corner from Berkeley Square. This was back in the early 1970s, when things were different.

Alex said [Scully now affecting a very plummy accent], 'Well, do help yourself to a bottle of champagne, my dear.' I'd been brought up super rough. The nearest I'd got to champagne before that was the Babycham we used to give our girlfriends before we embarked on a street fight. Babycham is not champagne. He left me in the gallery with the key and said, 'Drink all the champagne you want, my old dear, and pop the key through the letterbox on your way out.' He had given me the key to his gallery and all his trust – and all his champagne. I'm Irish, you know, so I made good use of the champagne. I was in the gallery alone with the work of all the people I admired, particularly Paul Huxley. There were a few works by Bridget Riley around, Phillip King, Barry Flanagan, Michael Craig-Martin... These people were very senior to me, and I admired them all. Paul Huxley used to use beautiful colours. I remember he used these strange, wonderful green colours. He had a fantastic sense of colour. Paul and I subsequently became friends. I mean, he was the one who got me to be an RA [Royal Academician], later in life. He's a wonderful guy.

Like Scully, Paul Huxley was something of a boy wonder who had attracted a great deal of attention when he finished art school. Seven years older than Scully, Huxley graduated from the Harrow School of Art in 1956 before attending the Royal Academy Schools from 1956 to 1960. Foreshadowing Scully's own itinerary, in 1965 he headed to America on a Harkness Fellowship, as Scully himself would do a decade later when he moved to New York. The sort of work Scully would have seen knocking around the Rowan Gallery, which Huxley also joined at a precocious age, would have chimed with his own inimitable take on abstraction, which seemed strenuously to yolk into a single plane the austerity of Mondrian and the scruffiness of Arshile Gorky. It is easy to see how Huxley's ambition to reconcile severe geometry, on the one hand, and loose gesture, on the other, would have appealed to Scully's mercurial and absorbent imagination.

Paul Huxley, *Untitled no. 128*, 1971

ss So there I was in this gallery. Can you imagine how I felt? I was 27 years old, and I was in the greatest gallery in London that had some incredible stars in it. Barry Flanagan, back then, was huge and made these fantastic soft sculptures, and he was such a nice guy too. I drank a bottle of champagne to celebrate, of course, and then I thought, 'Well, I'd better get to work.' Naturally I opened a second bottle of champagne to accompany the work. Because the first bottle of champagne was to celebrate the fairy tale that I was standing in the middle of, as the young prince, and the second was to go along with the work.

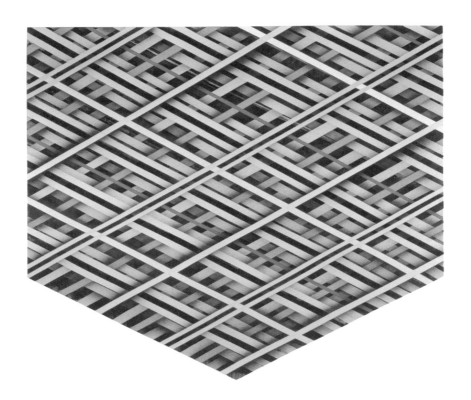

East Coast Light 2, 1973

KG You've got to do what you've got to do.

SS Behind the stretchers were triangles of wood that you would
    screw into the back of the frame, and that – to this day – is
    the way that the painting is secured. I now actually own
    that painting again. I got more and more drunk, of course.
    I remember throwing the triangles in the air with incredible
    happiness, and one of them I threw a bit too far. I watched
    with horror as it slowly spiralled through the air and landed
    in the worst way possible: it went through my painting –
    which was flipped over, flat on the carpeted floor – and
    stuck in the carpet underneath the painting. The carpet had
    assisted it by being soft. If the painting had been on a hard
    floor, the triangle would have bounced off the canvas but it
    actually made a hole in it. I didn't know quite what to do,
    so I just kind of ironed it out with my finger and hoped for
    the best. And you know what, nobody's ever found it, myself
    included. The painting is so busy, you don't see it. Those
    were my early days in London.

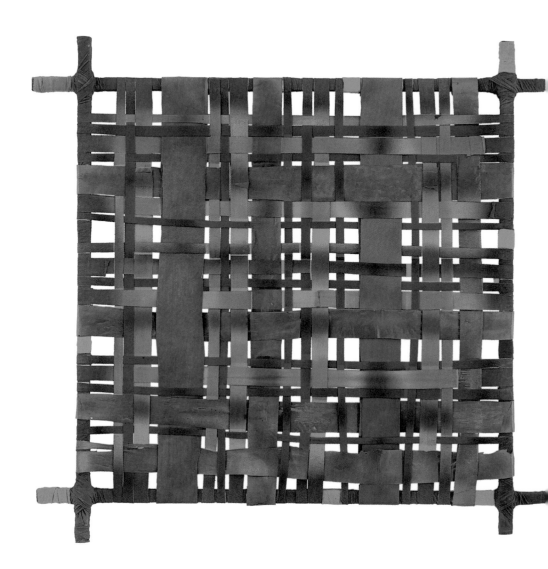

Harvard Frame Painting, 1972

CHAPTER FOUR

Blame

KG When did you decide to emigrate to America? You'd been to Harvard on a Frank Knox Fellowship, come back to England, joined the fabulous Rowan Gallery – 'the best in London' – and then resolved to head back to America. Why did you not stay in London?

Even as I spoke, I was aware that it is a question Scully has pondered many times. In an affectionate eulogy for a friend of his, the American art historian Alvin Martin, written in 2004, Scully compared his own deep sense of having been born far from where he truly belonged with that of his friend, whom he felt would have preferred to live in England. 'I came to America and glided across its bigness,' Scully wrote, 'for I too had been born in a place that was the wrong size. I moved like a whale in the ocean. I needed that space.'

SS I've often wondered about that. Billy Conn, who was a great light-heavyweight boxer, took Joe Louis, who was considered unbeatable, to thirteen rounds. He gave him a boxing lesson in thirteen rounds, and then he tried to knock him out, which of course you couldn't do against the hardest puncher in the world, and he got knocked out himself. At the end of the fight, someone asked him why he had done that, because he would have been world champion. His answer was: 'What's the point of being Irish if you can't be stupid?' I have often wondered about this, and why I went to New York to pick a fight with people I obviously wasn't qualified to prevail against. I mean, I didn't go to school with all the famous art critics. I didn't go to school with the famous collectors, or the famous curators who were going to be the famous museum directors. I wasn't stitched in. For some bizarre reason, not even known to me, I decided I would go to America as a kind of dare, I suppose. Because I thought it was the most difficult thing I could do, and I'm very attracted to difficulty. Why that is, I'm not sure. It's a little like the studio with the 20-ft-diameter hole in the middle of it: it's quite dangerous to make a painting in that room.

KG Was it just too easy in London then?

SS Yeah, I suppose I found it too easy-going. Even now, I have great affection for London. I adore England. I'm not one of those Irish people that doesn't like the English or doesn't like England. I love Ireland, of course – it's my home country. But I do love England, and I've met many wonderful people in England.

I'll tell you another story now. I know you like my stories. Don't pretend you don't! I was going up to Newcastle, and I was staying with my grandparents. My grandparents lived at 56 Hallgarth Street in Durham. They had an outside toilet, you know, you went with a flashlight. My grandad was from the north of England. He had been a coal miner all his life. He was the most beautiful man. My grandmother was Scottish. I had to get to Durham from London, but I had hardly any money so I went up on the bus. I had to choose between going to Newcastle or Sunderland because the bus didn't stop at Durham. The ticket guy said to me, 'You want to go to Newcastle or Sunderland?' and I was thinking, 'Newcastle, Sunderland, Newcastle, Sunderland... Sunderland, Newcastle, uh... Newcastle, no Sunderland!' because Sunderland was a bit cheaper.

So I get out at Sunderland, but it's one o'clock in the morning, and there's nothing. I start walking aimlessly towards Durham, which is impossible because it's miles, in the pitch black. A dog comes and bites me on the leg – a farm dog. That starts me crying. I sat there eating my pork pie, because in those days I ate meat, feeling sorry for myself (although not as sorry for myself as the pig that was in the pork pie). So I'm walking along. It's about 2:30 in the morning. I've got my thumb out and a car stops. A guy picks me up and takes me to his apartment, where his wife is asleep. The Olympic Games were on, and we stayed up watching them together. He had a collection of – what should I call it? – railing art. You know, the kind of art you buy on the street – schlock art, basically. He had this first-class collection of terrible art all over the apartment, and he wondered if it was valuable. It was the most extraordinary situation.

He was so kind to me, incredibly nurturing and hospitable. In the morning he made me breakfast and took me to the railway station. He had given up his sleep for me because normally he would go home and sleep, and he waited until the first train came in the morning. The train was on a narrow-gauge railway and passed all the slag heaps in the Northeast. It gradually filled with young boys who all looked the same, as if they were out of *Brave New World*, carrying a sandwich tin and dressed in dark blue, going to the slag heaps, the remnants of the mines. And there I was, the art student, sitting among a sea of 16-year-old boys who were going to work.

I've experienced a lot of kindness in England. I think English people are extremely empathetic. They don't just let you lie on the floor like they do in New York.

KG Yet ultimately you abandoned England for the USA and, in particular, New York. After so much to-ing and fro-ing, back and forth from Harvard to London, from London to New York, what tipped the balance?

SS Yeah, it's a very interesting question, and it indicates a certain equivocation on my part. One thing I would say is that in

1974 I was shown by a guy called Louis Leithold in LA. That was the first place I showed outside London.

KG And where you had your first catalogue.

SS Yeah, and the interesting thing is that there was a natural correspondence between the phenomenological issues in LA art, like Larry Bell and his beautiful smoky boxes or Robert Irwin's issues with light, and the more optical aspects of abstract painting that were being practised in England by Tess Jaray, Peter Sedgley and Bridget Riley. So, that was a more obvious connection. I liked LA enormously, and I loved the West Coast, but I just couldn't stretch the umbilical cord far enough. I could not countenance an eleven-hour flight. I simply couldn't deal with it psychologically because I knew that I had to keep returning to Mother Europe, or Mother London, or Mother Paris; because I need all this, and it's where I'm from. Even though I like the openness of America, I come from the density of Europe. So I settled on New York as a compromise because New York is really, in a certain sense, an outpost of Europe. It's where so many people go, and you hear all these European accents when you're in New York that you don't hear in LA.

I actually love the LA accent. It's much closer to the British accent. It doesn't have quite the twang on it that the New York accent has. I love the flat way that they speak. I have friends in LA, particularly Andy Moses, who's the son of Ed Moses and a very good friend. I've such a sweet relationship with Andy. I was made very welcome on the West Coast in a way that I wasn't in New York. In New York I had to fight, so I kept going back. On occasion, I would equivocate about my decision and have doubts about staying in New York because it was so brutal.

KG Do you think that brutality, having something to kick against, was critical not only to the way the work turned out, but also how important it turned out to be?

Sean Scully in his Duane Street studio, New York, 1980

ss I've had this conversation a number of times with friends and the answer is: I don't know. But my friends seem to know. They seem to think it's very important. There's no question that paintings like *Backs and Fronts*, of course, and *Enough*, *Heart of Darkness* and *Adoration* were combative portraits of the city; or a painting like *Blame*, which is in the Whitney Museum now, is really a picture that's, in a sense, blaming itself. I do view New York, and Manhattan in particular, as a city of transaction and culpability. During the pandemic, it's been borne out by the bad feeling between the inhabitants of the city. They're not pulling together as they do in other cities – as they do in London, for example, where we have the Leader of the Opposition being quite kind to the Prime Minister. This wartime sense that you get in England of people being on each other's side and helping each other, and helping old people – bringing them shopping, all that kind

Heart of Darkness, 1982

Adoration, 1982

Blame, 1983

of stuff – you don't get that in America, particularly in New York. What you get in New York is blame. The city seems to run on envy and blame. The question is: is that necessary for great art? In the past, centres of great art, like Venice, were hotbeds of intrigue and blame, so I suppose, in a sense, the long-term answer is probably yes.

KG Okay, but putting art to one side, what kind of a place has it been to spend a sizable portion of your life? This hotbed of 'blame', 'envy' and 'intrigue' has been your principal residence now for more than four decades.

SS It was very rewarding in many ways. I can't say I didn't have a lot of good times. I've had some wonderful memories in New York, and I've had some very good friends too, particularly Arthur Danto and Deborah Solomon. My early supporter Charles Choset, who died in the AIDS epidemic, was a great friend. I can't answer these questions very well in retrospect, to be honest. New York was extraordinarily engaging, that I can certainly say. And I had artist friends who are people I admired greatly, like Robert Ryman and Robert Mangold. I thought they were doing great art.

KG You mention Ryman, as you have many times, and I've often meant to ask you about his influence. I know you've said elsewhere that his work had a purity to it that, in the end, you felt hit too few notes.

I had in mind some comments that Scully had made at a lecture at Harvard in 1992. Reflecting on his relationship with minimalism, he said, 'I think something happened that wasn't so great at a certain point with American formalism and American minimalism. There are certainly some very wonderful post-minimalist paintings being made. I'm a great admirer of Robert Ryman's work, but at the same time it's a bit like trying to play music with

Angel, 1983

Come In, 1983

Heat, 1984

a penny whistle. You've got such a narrow range, and you can hit so few notes. What I'd like to do is to open it up mentally.'

KG Were you consciously thinking about notions of purity, and whether or not there was sufficient human complication at the time when you were making your transition from minimalism to the more expressive work?

SS Yeah, in a sense, that's *the* question. You know, one doesn't always know why one is doing something. You get led along by life and you are navigating, but you're also being directed by unfathomable forces and coincidences. I loved Ryman's and also Agnes Martin's work, and I still do. However, I am aware that the admiration I felt did not correspond to the mission that I discovered for myself. I probably had an inkling of that (though not a fully rounded understanding) before I went. But I'm willing to go on a hunt, or as my dear, loving friend Arthur Danto said about me, 'There's never much space between Sean's ideas and his actions.' I always thought that was a beautiful way of describing me. I don't have much hesitation or fear. So I had a hunch I had to go there and take something on, but I wasn't exactly sure what it was. The severity of the paintings that I made when I first was there was very appealing to me, as was the work of Bob Ryman, whom I was extremely fond of.

I am aware that the work of an artist like Ad Reinhardt or even Rothko achieves its greatness through extreme focus, which implies equivalent sacrifice. What I wanted to do, of course, was open art up, not close it down further for the sake of intensity. The great danger in opening it up is the loss of intensity, and the loss of integrity or the image of integrity, let's say, for something bigger and more popular – something that's capable of holding the attention of a bigger audience. So that's obviously what I pursued, with more formal elements, metaphor, a rougher sense of material, changes in scale, literary references – which all bring me, in a certain sense, closer to Jasper Johns. Johns is another artist I've admired greatly, particularly early on when he was making work that could be compared with the apparent banality of somebody like Philip Glass, the composer, by painting numbers – but painting them like Cézanne, and that fascinated me.

KG During this kind of prolonged transition that occurred in the early 1970s when you were sometimes in England, sometimes in America, you were teaching on occasion in both places. What about teaching? You've had a number of positions, teaching fine art – in London at the Chelsea College of Arts and at Goldsmiths, and in the States at Princeton University and at Parsons School of Design in New York. Did it help or get in the way?

SS I was in two minds about it. One can argue that to teach is to learn. You're learning about yourself, and you're learning about other people, so it does expand you in a certain way. But in another way, you're giving something away that you need for your own art. If you say that art requires great intensity and solitude, then of course you're giving that away. I mean, I don't remember Cézanne teaching, but I do remember him walking up Sainte-Victoire every day till it nearly killed him. The people who did teach a lot seemed to be somewhat less focused.

KG Did it divert your focus?

SS To some degree, yes. What one has to avoid at all costs is the sacrifice of liberty and the promotion in its stead of compromise and reasonableness. Because art is not about that. Art is an extreme manifestation of a thought or a feeling, or a combination of both. I didn't want to get into a situation where I became a committee person. I've been asked to be

Cimabue, *Madonna Enthroned with the Child,*
Saint Francis and Four Angels, c. 1278–80

on committees and I've always refused because I do feel that they would suck the energy out of me; or they would make me somehow more civilized, and I don't want to be civilized. I think, in a way, to make paintings, particularly the kind of paintings I make, you have to have a lot of animal energy in you. I remember reading about Cimabue. It was said that Cimabue was difficult and he's a great artist, of course. And I wrote a nice piece on Cimabue.

In 2010 Scully wrote a prose sketch on the 13th-century Florentine painter. 'His work', Scully noted, 'is emotionally dense and very impacting – in the sense of the violence of it.' Attracted almost as much to the irascibility of the figure as he is to the often overlooked mastery of his painting, which was largely eclipsed by the fame of his contemporary Giotto (who, according to the 16th-century artist and writer Giorgio Vasari, was also Cimabue's pupil), Scully observed that 'there's a savagery about his work. Part of this was the product of his personality. He was, by all accounts, very difficult and unforgiving. He was a disobedient, renegade figure. In other words, the kind of person that we got used to round about the time of the High Renaissance, which was a change from the more obedient and reverential souls that had come before him. He was a revolutionary from the inside.'

ss I always thought this disobedience was necessary. You cannot be too politic. I couldn't be a trustee of the Tate, for example. I've been invited to be a trustee of this and that, and I've never agreed. I just feel it's dangerous.

Detail from *Aran*, 2005

CHAPTER FIVE

Falling Wrong

KG In your early years, how important was your Irish identity? Or is this something that evolved over time?

This is a question I've been meaning to ask for some time. Whenever I see Scully in Dublin, his sense of 'Irishness' emerges naturally as a topic of conversation. But does he feel it strongly elsewhere? There is a poetic meditation that Scully wrote in 2002 on the subject of one of his best-known series of works, 'Wall of Light' (an ongoing series of paintings begun in the late 1990s whose origin and meaning we would find ourselves discussing at great length in a later conversation), which suggests how deeply woven into the patterns of his imagination his Celtic roots came to be. 'I had been thinking about the history of Ireland,' Scully wrote of the inception of this series. 'I wanted to make [...] a monument that connected the ancient Irish walls, the black and white of façades in Ireland, and ultimately the present in one monumental stone object. To make something simultaneously ancient and contemporary: that pushed out, psychologically, the long period of colonization of this country by compressing time. A stone wall, made solid, like stone walls in Ireland made a thousand years ago, when Ireland was a country of light and a cradle of the arts. My deepest wish was to manifest solid in stone the light of our present hope, and our future possibility. A wall of light.' I was keen to find out when Scully became conscious of that invigorating energy of Irishness with which his imagination was hardwired.

SS I think it became stronger over time. It became apparent to me that I was very Irish. There's something intemperate

Arran, 1986

Arran, 1990

Wall of Light Arran, 2002

about me, and I'm very passionate. I remember one summer I was in somebody's house in Ireland, having dinner, and I just thought, 'This is continental. This isn't northern Europe. These people are hot.' Irish music, of course, is a driving force in my life, and when I came across Beckett I thought I'd lose my mind with happiness.

For an article that Scully contributed to the catalogue for 'Objet Beckett', an exhibition at the Centre Pompidou in 2007 devoted to the Irish novelist and playwright, Scully recalled his first encounter with Beckett – a performance of *Waiting for Godot*, which he attended while in art school. 'As it unfolded I thought I was in paradise,' Scully wrote. 'It was true, it was hard and it was unflinching.' Scully would come to see in Beckett a companionable form, one who saw minimalism as a means for intensifying the experience of life. 'Some people like to see Beckett in terms of minimalism. But this is an Irish minimalism, which is not very minimal. It's austere. So is Ireland. So is its story. And in his special way Beckett is a storyteller. It's the line that goes back onto and into itself. It's the system of rage and mystery.'

KG When did you discover Beckett?

SS When I was at Newcastle. I've kind of educated myself on the hoof as I've gone. I didn't really have a formal education when I was young, so there are a lot of holes in my education. I hang out with people who are more educated than me, like you, so that I can get educated. My friends have helped fill in some of the holes.

I remember when we lived on the Old Kent Road, my mother had a fight with a big Polish woman who was beating her up on the street, and I grabbed this lady round the legs and made her fall over. I was only four, but even then I was a bit of a scrapper. I said, 'Don't you hit my mummy,' and my mother was able to escape a serious thrashing.

THE DIRE FIRE OF IRE
OF IRELAND
THE DIRE IRE OF IRELAND
OF DIRE FIRE OF IRE

DIRE FIRE IRE

Handwritten page, 'The Dire Fire'

The Old Kent Road was unbelievably trashy, still is, espe-cially where we lived. When we moved to Islington, to Highbury, which was really an Irish ghetto, it became obvi-ous to me that I was quite Irish. My grandmother was deeply Irish, deeply religious. All the people I knew were Irish, and I went to a Catholic school that had a lot of Irish and Polish kids. You had all these itinerant workers coming over to stay at my granny's house. And the priests who were com-ing over to teach at the school, many of them were Irish. So I was in a very Irish milieu, you know. Except for Vick, the cross-dressing comedian who lived in the next room and was Jewish.

Then I kind of forgot about it again because I moved to sunny Sydenham in south London. I was really integrated into English society. I considered myself a Londoner. But as I got older, I found I had a very powerful attraction to Irish literature and Irish ways of thinking. There is something ancient in me that's very attracted to Druid sites and sim-ple, essential forms. And then I began to visit Ireland, and the relationship became stronger and stronger until, in the end, it won out over the relationship with England – in part, because the Irish embraced me with a great passion. I do have what I would call a careless nature, and that does seem quite Irish. I feel very comfortable when I'm there.

KG   When did you start showing in Ireland?

SS   That's when I first showed at Trinity [College, Dublin], at the art gallery there. That would have been in '81.

KG   Was it called the Douglas Hyde then?

SS   It was called the Douglas Hyde. I remember when I was 14, I think, or 13, there was a school trip to Ireland. I desper-ately wanted to go, so that means I felt it very strongly back

Sean Scully, the hills of Wicklow, June 1983

then – that I should go home. I remember my mother put down a £2 deposit. That was a lot of money.

I was a chronic bedwetter. I had all this Victorian paraphernalia to 'cure' me of this ailment, in the way that dogs were cured from making pee-pees on the carpet; they had their noses rubbed into it and then they learned not to do it. Well, I had all this electricity in my bed like a Frankenstein movie set – bells going off in the middle of the night, metal sheets with holes in them, all that Victorian kind of stuff. And I had a chart above my bed with 'D' and 'W'. Eventually I had to admit that I could not 'cure' myself in time to go to Ireland. Of course, as soon as I escaped my parents I stopped within twenty-four hours.

So, back then, the 'Irishness' was obviously an issue. And if I'd gone on that trip, I think it would have manifested itself quite powerfully because my relationship with Ireland has

Inisheer, 1990–96

become very strong. When I'm in Ireland people do relate to me very strongly, and I to them.

KG There's a real affection there.

SS Yeah, there's a great love.

KG Like Beckett, you've managed to compound your Irishness with life and work elsewhere. In fact, it's that elsewhere that has arguably intensified the Irishness. For him, the else-where was France. For you, it was England and then America. At some point, Germany too will come into play. When does that come about?

SS A very dear friend of mine – an Israeli artist called Michael Gitlin, a wonderful sculptor – introduced me to a German art dealer. Her name was Schmela. She walked into my stu-dio and said, 'I have to show this work in Düsseldorf,' and that started my love affair with Germany, which has become more profound over time. I'm very interested in Germany because it was the home of philosophy in the 19th century. And then of course with Nazism it lost its mind. That is somewhat inscrutable to me: how a culture that is so pro-found and great and humanistic could go so awry. But you can see the same thing being a distinct possibility in America with Donald Trump, with fascism, intolerance, racism and blame – that magic word – always ready to rear their heads. In Germany, of course, people were actually burning money to keep warm, whereas in America a despot, or a wannabe despot, like Donald Trump can't do that because there are too many checks in place. But I can see how, if the circum-stances were stripped away economically, somebody would have to get the blame. In the case of America it would be the Mexicans, whereas in Germany Hitler nominated the Jews. Somebody has to get the blame when fascism rears its head. It can't be introspective or flexible or dialectic. It's pure brute force. Germany is a country that is utterly committed to redemption, and one way it is doing that is through art. Of course, you know, the fascists always kill the artists because the artists are the enemy. Artists are the ones who encourage people to think subversively, to be disobedient and, worst of all, imaginative. Flexibility of mind, curiosity and tolerance are all enemies of totalitarian thinking.

KG Just as Ireland embraced you, so has Germany. Why is that, do you think? It has always seemed to me that your work is striving for some kind of balance, trying to find order out of the chaos. Do you think a perceived compatibility of spirit in that respect lies at the heart of the symbiosis?

SS You know, Nietzsche believed that reason and emotion should have the freedom to coexist. It's not necessary to compromise on either one. And that, I thought, was very interesting in relation to my own work, which is extremely structural but also emotional – or the treatment of it is very emotional. It's a structure that includes tolerance. It's not dominating in the way that I would say minimalism is. Minimalism doesn't really take any prisoners; it doesn't allow for many ways of thinking. It seems to me extremely didactic, whereas my work is open to a lot of readings.

KG The allegation is that minimalism is coercive and that it tries to cleanse itself of the human. You've let the human back in.

SS I've insisted on human dirt. As I sometimes say jokingly, some of my paintings look as if they've been slept in. In performances of Beckett, you know, all the old overcoats are kind of dirty, and in my work there's a lot of dirty colour.

KG No purity.

June 07

I agree with Nietsche – we have our invention and nothing more. It's true because we think it's true. Our sense of structure is subjective. Art though, in our attempt to create our own nature, it's a terrible, rediculous, and profoundly beautiful arrogance. And nothing is more arrogant than a small painting.

Handwritten page, 'I Agree with Nietsche', 2007

ss No, there's no purity there at all. In fact, I was asked in an interview once if I could think of a single word to describe my idea of creativity, and before the person had finished the question I'd thought of the answer: impurity. Impurity is the enemy of purity. And purity is always the best friend of fascism. So there I go again, I'm always at it. I'm absolutely committed to the fragile preservation of a kind of tolerant architecture, one might say. Or complex architecture. One that includes wrongness. As you know, I oddly titled a painting of mine *Falling Wrong*. Someone said to me, 'Why the hell did you call it *Falling Wrong*?' And I said, 'Well, it's more interesting than *Falling Right*, because there's only one way to fall right but there are a thousand ways to fall wrong.' So wrongness and difficulty are always very interesting to me.

Falling Wrong, 1985

The relationship between the searching rhetoric of Scully's titles and the bold solidity of the works to which they are attached is an intriguing layer to his craftsmanship. The two elements – one verbal and the other visual – riff off each other to create an elastic logic, an amplifying ambiguity that reinforces the sense that these are paintings that are as irresolvable as they are steadfast in their quest for resolution. 'The titles are very important to me,' Scully said in a lecture at the National Gallery of Art in Washington, DC, in 2007, 'and are a little crazy. I'm not referring to anything that's got much to do with order. So, what I'm doing, in a sense, is misusing the language of order. *Falling Wrong* seems like something that could be out of Beckett but it's not. But it has the same kind of attitude. Falling wrong is better than falling right, so to speak. And falling wrong is interesting. So the wrongness in the painting is as interesting as the rightness.'

ss It's how the world is made, isn't it? The world is made up of relationships that are difficult, but at the same time that doesn't mean to say they're not positive, or they shouldn't be supported. These thought processes run through my work, or through my thinking, constantly. I suppose you might say it's my religion. I feel so connected to it. It's the way I live all the time.

KG There's a muscular music to the work that seems always to be wrestling for harmony – a melody amongst the dirt, impurity and chaos.

ss Yeah, the layering of the work gives the colours a kind of difficulty. It gives the work a sense of mystery about how they got there, and how they got into their body – how that colour rides in that body in this world. As opposed to just painting things flat. That probably appeals to the sense of layering that's in German culture, but it also appeals to the Italian sensibility. I've noticed this a lot: that this sense of layering of identity and difficulty of naming what something is, in a technical sense, forces you into a kind of flexibility. Because if you can't name it you can't finish it off, you can't terminate it, so it has the ability to come back again. As Albert Einstein said, when you know what something is you don't have to think about it any more. It's a dead thing. It has lost all its mystery. In a sense, it has been conquered.

I always thought the work of Andy Warhol was very banal. It doesn't interest me at all. I was at the Whitney when his retrospective was on, and I didn't even bother getting off on that floor. Not that I have anything against Warhol. As a person I don't admire him, but the work I'm indifferent to. However, I do think that the misregistration in Warhol is what makes it fascinating, which goes back to the same thing about difficulty. When something's right, it's difficult for it to fascinate. Part of the reason why Beuys is so interesting to people, including myself, is the difficulty of it – the fine balance of it in relation to its massive physicality. The delicacy of the thinking in relation to the weight of the material is very interesting to me. In Warhol, the fact that the images are always misregistered gives the painting its lifeblood because it's never right. I know from being an apprentice that in printmaking you're not supposed to misregister; you're supposed to get the registration right. With a Warhol its energy comes from the fact that it's banal on the one hand and misregistered on the other.

KG Yes, but once you understand that tension, once you've got the joke, it kills the energy of it.

SS I'm personally not interested in Warhol, but I do understand why people like it. What's really fascinating to me is that Arthur Danto, who in New York was like my father and protected me, had two favourite artists. One was Andy Warhol, the other was me. [Laughing] I've never been able to figure out why we were his two favourite artists because we seem to stand for such opposite values. But one thing that does unify us, of course, is that we use banal subject matter. A stripe is banal. The stripe is everywhere. You've got it all over your shirt, and I've got it on my shirt. And yet I've taken something that is already killed by society as an image, and I've used this to create what I hope is humanistic, engaging, moving art. What Warhol does is take pictures of things that are actually kind of worn out, and the emptiness of it is its depth, one might say, if one wanted to be semantically clever. The banality of what I took is, in a sense, the underlying strength of my work. I've never deviated from that. I don't allow my work to get too fancy. I always keep it somehow archetypal, using archetypal shapes like a square or a rectangle, and never let it get baroque or decorative. This, I think, is really profound in my work.

It is true, of course, that Scully and Warhol do share a fascination with banal subject matter. Whereas for Scully it is the ubiquitous stripe, for Warhol it is the retail commodity of a soup can or the Brillo boxes found in every supermarket. But the similarities between the two artists break down almost as quickly as they are identified. At the heart of Warhol's work is a preoccupation with the mechanics of mass production. He famously said that he wanted to be a machine. For Scully, however, unique craftsmanship is crucial. Every stripe attests to the moment in which it, and it alone, was brushed into being by fossilizing gesture. It is an aspect of Scully's work that I've always admired, and I wanted to know where that impulse stemmed from – to resist the allure of automation that had caught both Pop Art and minimalism in the teeth of its gears.

ss I found those early number paintings by Jasper Johns very attractive. I saw a definite correlation there. On the one hand he was painting serialization and numeration, but he was

Jasper Johns, *o through 9*, 1961

painting it like a wannabe European, like an old master. He was painting something as banal as a number as if it were an object of beauty, which of course is a little bit related to what [the 18th-century French painter Jean-Baptiste-Siméon] Chardin did when he showed that you can just paint a bowl of fruit. And relatively speaking, it was as radical as Chardin was shocking to people. Chardin didn't try to paint pictures of battleships or mountains or popes or princes. He painted apples in a bowl next to a jug. This is, in a sense, compressing time, the equivalent of what Johns was doing. I thought that Chardin struck a beautiful balance between what was ordinary and what was elevated. I've maintained that kind of thinking in my work all the way through.

As Scully finished making the point that he had endeavoured 'all the way through' his work to reconcile into a single aesthetic

Jean-Baptiste-Siméon Chardin, *A Bowl of Plums*, c. 1728

surface an awareness of what is 'ordinary' and what is 'elevated', I couldn't help wondering how that ambition was pursued and achieved in other forms into which he has channelled his creative energy, beyond the making of paintings per se. After all, rightly or wrongly, paintings often carry with them the connotation of something being portrayed – a reality or truth that exists outside the edges or frame of the work. In recent years, sculpture – which depends on entirely different laws of physics and visual expectations – has become an increasingly important element in Scully's work. At what point, I wondered, did he begin thinking about sculpture, and was it, for him, aligned with or separate from the project of painting?

ss   I remember making a sculpture when I was a student in Newcastle. It was an old mattress – a miner's mattress. I painted it different colours and wove wire through it, but I found the physicality of it burdensome because, in a sense, I was trying to make it pictorial. It's a coloured mattress sprung – the metal from the inside of it all painted up different colours. It looks like a floating Impressionist painting. So sculpture was there; I always had an interest in it. I do like its immediacy. Another thing I really love about sculpture is this: nobody says, 'What's that?' It comes back to the same old issue again: how do you three-dimensionalize a two-dimensional diagram? Which is what a painting is.

KG   Right. Everybody always assumes that a painting is *of* something else...

ss   ...that would be three-dimensional.

KG   That would be three-dimensional. It's never the thing itself. But I've always felt that to appreciate your work properly, one has to understand it is the *Ding an sich*, it is 'the thing itself'. It's not trying to be another thing.

The Sculpture.

my Sculpture is always a block.
The giant sculpture in Aix-en-provence
is a WALL OF LIGHT CUBED. So that, the
physical and conceptual argument of the
work, is consistent without and within. So
that, the inside is the same as the
outside. So that, when looking at the
outside of the block, one can feel the inside
without being able to see it. One can trust
that it is made with a truth to materiality
that is organized consistently throughout.

I have written on the ancient walls of ARAN.
These are dry-stone walls, where each stone
is fitted into place, by sound and by touch.
However, this feeling, for material can be
applied to all ancient walls and blocks
that are 'fitted' into place forever. From
Mexico to Egypt to Cambodia.

The drawing in my sculpture is carried
through to create a feeling of inevitability
and utter contentment. Knowing that
something is exactly what it appears to be,
and not a simple appearance or facade.

In a way, these are the opposite of most other sculpture. They are not a narrative arrangement, but a massive abstract figure, that compresses time and the weight of material, in a cubed drawing. By pushing out space, I want to push out time = to offer an enduring now.

Sean Henley

June 22 09

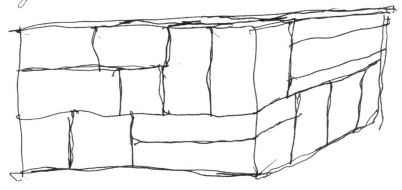

Handwritten page, 'The Sculpture', 2009

ss   People still have an issue with this, which is extraordinary really since abstraction has been around for over a hundred years.

KG   Do you feel that people react to your sculpture in a more immediate way than your paintings?

ss   Yeah. They understand it in a more immediate sense because it's already a thing. We are things. We are walking around. We are bodies and we are objects.

KG   You remove the chimera of mimesis.

ss   I absolutely love looking at paintings. I sometimes joke that my sculpture is kind of like Donald Duck taking one of my paintings and just turning it into a sculpture. If you took one of my paintings and made it into a sculpture, you'd actually have one of my sculptures. So I didn't have to mess around at all to make sculptures. They made themselves. All I had to do is make my paintings three-dimensional and I had sculptures.

CHAPTER SIX

Backs and Fronts

KG Your first show in New York was in 1977...

SS Yeah, at a gallery that lasted four months.

KG What's the story there?

SS I went to the Pace Gallery to try and have a show there. Of course, they weren't interested in me because I was nothing. David Gibbs, however, was interested in me. He left Pace because he had had enough of the founder of Pace, Arnold Glimcher, telling him to smile. So Gibbs opened his own gallery, which was not successful. I had to build the damn thing. I think they had four exhibitions. One of them was Catherine Lee. It was on the corner of Spring Street and West Broadway. There was a gallery from Berlin in the same building, one of the first intrusions into New York from Europe. In that gallery Joseph Beuys was sitting with his coyote as I was going up and down with these pieces of Sheetrock, or plasterboard as they call it in Europe, to build the gallery upstairs, two floors above.

KG So when you say you built the gallery, you literally built the gallery?

SS That's what New York was like. That symbolized it for me. It took my body and my soul to stay there. Art takes everything. I think Picasso said something like that. What does it take to be a famous artist? The answer is: it takes everything. What does it take to be a failed artist? Same answer. Art is a rum business, as Turner said. You've got to be up for it. I carried all those pieces of Sheetrock there. I put all the walls up. I painted it. I did the whole damn thing. The gallery was beautiful. I had a review in the *New York Times*; very interesting, because to get a review in the *New York Times* was unusual. It was by John Russell, who was an extremely generous, positive art critic. He later wrote a very beautiful review of Rauschenberg and Johns, who were on at the same time, and he called it Mr. Outside and Mr. Inside. He wrote a fantastic review of my show.

The review, excavated from the archive of the *New York Times*, helpfully chronicles how Scully's work was already resonating. 'The basic motif of Mr. Scully's paintings', Russell wrote, 'is a long narrow bar of pigment less than half an inch broad. Now alive in the light, now resolutely matt, Mr. Scully's bars play off one variant of given color against another in such way that the whole room vibrates softly and yet briskly. Sometimes a single square panel holds these vibrations in check; sometimes two panels are set side by side, with a subtle pairing that puts us in mind of other forms of mating. Either way, this is a very distinguished show. Vivat Scully, and Gibbs!' In spite of Russell's enthusiasm for both the artist and the dealer, the exhibition proved an inauspicious start for Scully and Gibbs, with the gallery closing a season later.

ss I sold a work on paper to a guy called Charles Choset, who became an extremely dear friend. He used to buy work on a very informal basis. He lived in a fifth-floor walk-up on Bedford Street that was so small you couldn't swing a cat in it. It was jammed with art, and he had a library that was two deep – you know, there was a library behind a library. He knew every single book in the library. He had a very strong preference for Edith Wharton, but he was just about the most well-read person I've ever met in my life. He was extraordinary. He died of AIDS eventually.

For Charles Choset, 1988

Charles Choset at Scully's Duane Street studio, New York, 1981

KG You made a very beautiful elegiac painting for him – *For Charles Choset.*

SS I was the last person to see him alive. It absolutely broke my heart when he died. I thought I would have a nervous breakdown. I used to shave him in hospital. He used to look at me adoringly while I shaved him because he was obviously in love with me. I got the call that he had slipped into a kind of coma, but he had been in semi-comas and come out of them again. I remember walking into the room and there was a very lovely nurse who said 'the family is here', and that was it. It just broke me up so bad. I walked in and I held his hand and told him that I'd got all my work back, because his apartment was jammed with my work. And I told him that everything was taken care of and I loved him. As soon as I said I loved him, he flatlined. That is really interesting about the human will: the issue of love and the power of love, which nobody can quantify. It's often been muddled

1982 #4, 1982

up with sentimentality, which it is not connected to. He was in that coma for four days, waiting for me to show up so that he could go away. That absolutely smashed me up.

When I became famous at the beginning of the '80s – '81, '82, '83 – I was *the* abstract painter in New York. When I made all those paintings where I broke everything up and put emotion back into abstraction, which has been well documented – by you, among others. But then my son Paul died, and Charles died. Charles was really like a brother to me. We were extraordinarily close. We used to drink screwdrivers. Those screwdrivers really screwed us up, I have to say. And he would play records. He had a great interest in music and would get all the latest records. He had a lot of stuff for such a poor person. He was as poor as a church mouse.

As Scully reminisced about New York in the early 1980s, his memory humid with heartache and music, anguish and acclaim, I was aware that there was a gap in our conversation. So far we had only touched on the milestone 'manifesto' work that had propelled him to prominence: *Backs and Fronts*. Crammed tight with the city's complex rhythms and architecture, the eleven sections that make up the painting changed the way that Scully's work was perceived not only by others, but also by himself. I knew that to appreciate Scully's art and his imagination's incubation in New York fully, it was essential to understand that painting. It felt like the right time to find out more.

KG   I'd love to know more about the story of *Backs and Fronts*, which set the stage for so much of what would transpire for you in the 1980s in New York. I remember you once saying that the painting began life as a smaller work – one that was in conversation with Picasso's *Three Musicians* of 1921.

SS   That's right, and I thought it would be better to have four musicians because, you know, I'm steeped in the history of

BACKS AND FRONTS

Backs and Fronts started out as
Four Musicians as an homage to
my friend Pablo Picasso who painted
Three Musicians – I didn't think that
3 panels or figures were enough for my
paintings – so I decided to call it 4
musicians. It stayed that way, with the
first four panels on the left locked together
side by side. Then however, I slowly added
more panels then more panels. As if more
and more musicians were joining an
already successful band – to make it
even better. So it became seven musicians
nine musicians then eleven musicians. And
finally after its long journey it was renamed
Backs and Fronts. Like figures or buildings
in a line. And if New york buildings being
tall stand like figures inhabited by human
figures. It made a strange new reality that
nobody could understand when I showed it at P.S. 1.
Though the musicians did, back in 1981.

S.S. N.Y. 2016

Handwritten page, 'Backs and Fronts', 2016

Pablo Picasso, *Three Musicians*, 1921

rock 'n' roll and there aren't many bands with three members. Bands usually have four members, and that would include U2 even. So I thought I'd make this painting and call it four musicians, and immediately I broke the rectangle.

By 'breaking the rectangle', Scully means that he had transgressed the rigid tradition of adhering to the confines of a parallelogram, or more specifically a rectangle or a square, in the construction of his work. By bolting together panels of varying widths and lengths, the ur-*Backs and Fronts* (provisionally entitled in the artist's mind *Four Musicians*) boldly adopted a ragged and irregular top and bottom border that was utterly at odds with painterly convention.

ss   At that time, my contemporaries and friends in New York were absolutely stuck in minimalism or process art – repeating brushstrokes or making geometric divisions that were relentlessly rational. And there it was. Of course, I'd been working up to this with other paintings like *Precious*...

KG *Araby*...

ss   *Araby* is a very important painting. You can see in *Araby* that I am going to do something. I remember asking several friends around to look at these paintings that I was making at the time and every single one of them was just bamboozled by what I was doing. *Backs and Fronts* had different styles in it: free colour, overpainting and, of course, these collisions. I took out the intermediary. And it had a kind of figurative metaphorical title and meaning. So, in other words, it broke a lot of rules that my colleagues were still obeying. I managed to make the painting by, in a sense, returning to Europe, because Picasso is European and I always loved his geometric figures, which were close to abstraction but never crossed the line. As it went on, I somehow got the courage

Precious, 1981

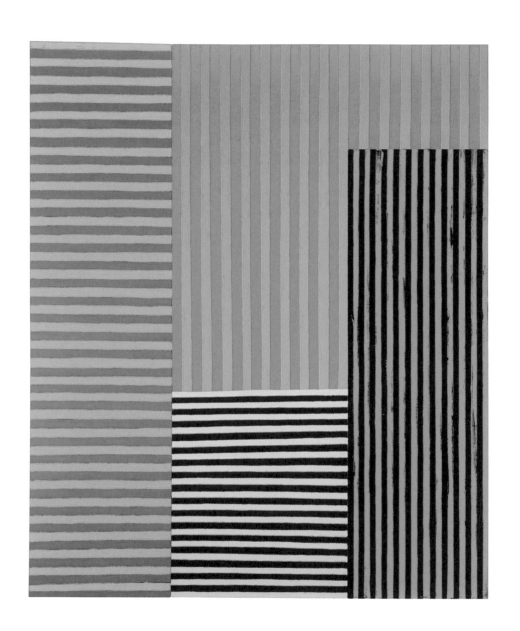

Araby, 1981

Fort #5, 1980–81

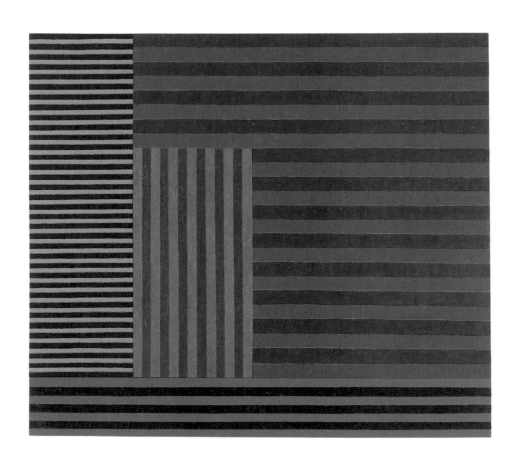

Come and Go, 1981

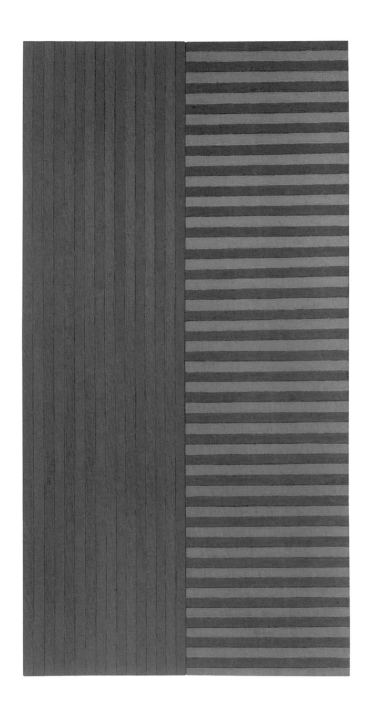

Firebird, 1980

to start expanding the work. And then I started expanding it stylistically until, by the end, it was thunderous. The eleven panels no longer had a relationship with a proper rectangle, and it was like a portrait of the city. I thought of New York as a city of collisions. That's what the painting was. The way that the city was slapped together was very visceral and I had been working in construction. I'd been framing out lofts, making all these windows and doorways and other people's lofts. This all was used in the painting.

KG What was the initial reaction?

SS The people who were involved in the visual arts didn't know what it was. There were six rooms in this exhibition ['Critical Perspectives', 1982] in PS1, which is part of MoMA. It was really, in New York, one of the two exhibitions of the decade. It was made by the relevant art critics of the day. I can't remember who they all were. And nobody was doing anything that would actually break the mould. They were pushing against the restraints of minimalism, but not breaking it. The people who loved my painting were the musicians.

KG The punks.

SS Yeah, because CBGB, where the Velvet Underground used to play, was just huge in New York, and I loved the Velvet Underground, of course. This incessant music, this overlaying music, these overlaying rhythms that were symptomatic of punk music – especially in the hands of Wire, who were a beautiful band – corresponded very well with what I was doing. So *Backs and Fronts* in particular – and there was another painting called *Enough* that's just jammed with information, like a subway map or something – was a painting about overload. My interest in rock 'n' roll, in popular music, which has been abiding, was very useful when I was

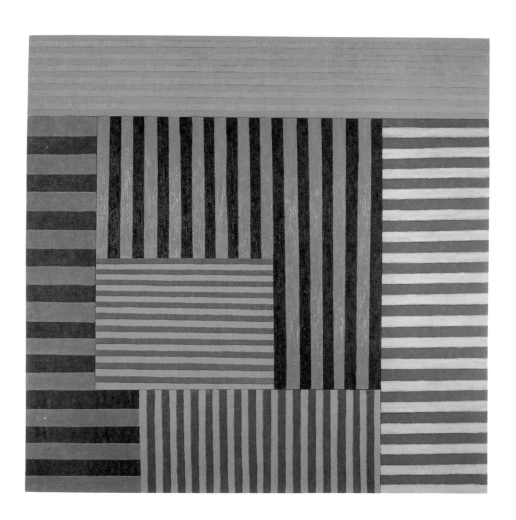

Enough, 1981

Bonin, 1982

A Day, 1982

Windows, 1980–81

making that painting. I was playing all this crazy music all the time, and it was working in harmony with what I was doing visually. Philip Glass was around too, you know, making an opera with three or four notes. The people who really understood the painting were those people.

There was a review of the show, however, and my painting was either illustrated or discussed, though not in particularly flattering terms. Joe Masheck, who was a hugely important critic at that time and had been the editor of *Artforum*, had all these notions about geometric painting. What he was doing, though, intellectually, wasn't really breaking with minimalism. It was dialoguing with its structure. So *Backs and Fronts* caused a lot of attention. It made noise. But it wasn't recognized as being important in the way that it has been since.

KG But you recognized that something had happened with the making of it...

SS Oh yeah, because I was working my way out of what I considered to be the minimalist prison. I had been relentlessly pushing against it for over a year, making *Blue*, *Come and Go*, *Araby*, *Precious* and *Fes* – all these paintings were pushing the limits of minimalism. With *Backs and Fronts*, I also broke the rectangle and turned it into a kind of sculptural painting, I suppose, so I recognize that it was a very big step.

CHAPTER SEVEN

Mexico Malloy

It's 11 May 2020, and Scully and I have arranged to talk again – our seventh recorded conversation since lockdowns were put in place by governments across the world in an effort to curb the spread of COVID-19. As I begin to set up my makeshift studio to capture our transatlantic telephone conversation – using a range of devices, including my wife's iPhone so we can see each other on FaceTime, my Android phone to record the sound, and an old SIMless smartphone with a different voice-recording app as back-up, just in case – I see that Scully has pinged me something on WhatsApp. It's a photo of a work he has just finished, still drying against the paint-spattered walls of his studio. The new work consists of bold blocks of burnished yellows and golds abutting slabs of midnight blue and inky-thick, primordial blacks. Built from big, quadrate stones of raging colour, puzzled perpendicularly, it is a painting that could only have come from Scully's brush. That is not to say it's echoless. It is as if a brickmaker has tipped Van Gogh's *Starry Night* into his spinning pugmill, mulched it to a mortar, and shoved the slabs of churned, intensified colour into his kiln. Scully pays tribute to the past by pulverizing it and forging something new. In the context of the unrelenting suffering and pain vibrating all around us as the pandemic's death toll continues to rise exponentially, Scully's resplendent work, to which he has attached the elegantly simple title *Star*, sounds a curiously buoyant note – a hopeful augury, pulsing as if from another world.

KG   That's a great painting.

SS   I'm so happy with it. I was thinking about Vincent, who was a big hero to me. The ingredients of Vincent are very special to

Star, 2020

Vincent van Gogh, *The Starry Night*, 1889

me. The appeal of Vincent is his clumsiness, and I was thinking about this recently. There's a lack of guile in this work. There's an incredible frontality to his work, a crudeness one might say, even though he was very urbane – lived in London, spoke English. You know, anybody who can speak a second language is urbane in my book, and that includes me now since I've smashed Spanish into my head, and I've got German wedged in halfway. [Laughing] So I'm upwardly mobile at my age, you know, 47, looking at that number in the mirror.

KG But there's more than merely a lack of guile in your brush-strokes that connects you to Van Gogh. You both make colour into something massive and bodily, and not just something that describes an object. You make colour the object.

SS That's a wonderful way to describe it. His paintings are almost like low-relief sculptures, aren't they?

KG Like a Braille for the eyes...

SS Yeah, it's a kind of Braille, and that appealed to me greatly because it shut down an area of interpretability; there wasn't much to translate. With Manet, whom I grew to adore later, there's a lot to translate. Manet is for a much more sophisticated eye or audience. I've come to believe that he's certainly the equal of Van Gogh, but he's not the first chapter for somebody who is trying to enter the world of art; Vincent can provide that.

Anyway, when I was making *Star*, I was of course thinking about [Vincent's] 'Starry, starry night', as Don McLean wrote in that wonderful song. The saturation of blues in *Starry Night* is fantastic. You know, I've been to Arles several times. I love Arles. I'm really nuts for it. Well, I'm just crazy about France. It really looks like the paintings. It's so great. You see Van Gogh paintings everywhere. You go into these

Arles Abend Vincent, 2013

little back streets, and there they are: Van Gogh paintings. He drew once and painted it like that, and you can see it. It appeals to the mind that's been educated by cartoons. The outlining of things which occurs, of course, in Walt Disney and comics – everything is outlined. It's emphatic. What you're looking at is not persuaded into reality. It's starkly insisted upon, you might say.

KG   In Van Gogh's paintings, all the different elements are kind of shoved up against each other. Even the spaces between things are shoved up against the things themselves. There's no room in any of the paintings. Everything's a thing shoved up against another thing. I know you've talked about this before, too.

SS   They're exhausting in a way.

KG   And you take something from that. People often talk about the abutment of your stripes and blocks. Forget Mondrian and Rothko, which are always the first two names people cite when they're describing your genealogy: The bloodline goes back to Van Gogh.

SS   Yes, it does. The thing with Rothko, of course, has been talked about a lot, but we're very different personalities. I'm much more physically aggressive than he is. He's a meditative and sedentary sort of person. You can get to Rothko if you combine Malevich and Turner. Everything comes out of something else.

KG   With you, it's as if Mondrian and Van Gogh had a love child.

SS   Yeah. There was a review of my work once that said these are paintings that don't leave you alone. I think the reviewer felt kind of molested. They are very insistent paintings, aren't they?

KG Well, did you want to make paintings that leave people alone?

SS Not really. But I didn't think about it all that much until now – now we're talking about Vincent and his hysterical insistence, that's the way I would describe it. This issue of putting down the colour always respecting that it's stuff, that it's substantive, is so important to me, and if I may say so I think it's the reason that painting keeps coming back.

KG We were talking about genealogies, and I remember you once suggested that a family tree could be drawn with roots and branches connecting Velázquez, Van Gogh and Mondrian. It's an unusual family tree...

SS I think my genealogy, or my family, is extremely unusual. And that, I think, is probably because I don't have any loyalties geographically. I can take from wherever I want because I'm not steeped in, for example, English painting, even though I've studied it. I know about Gainsborough and Reynolds, and the uncomfortable relationship they had. Of course, I'm on the side of Gainsborough in that one. At the same time I can take from the Quattrocento, and then I follow it to Spain. I even learned Spanish so that I could enter the culture. Most people who have a strong sense of national identity have ties to a particular idea of artistic evolution. But I don't. I just take it from wherever I want, and I find that so interesting, looking back. What I loved about Velázquez is the kind of raging restraint. I identify with the very emotional person who is also extremely structural, which I am. I'm both. I'm using that as a way of creating stress, I suppose. This goes back to the Van Gogh thing, doesn't it?

KG Is that part of the frustration – if that's the right word – that you have with Mondrian: there's too much restraint and not enough rage.

ss Yeah, I can't stay with Mondrian as an experience. However, I have to say that he's probably my biggest influence, because my adherence to horizontality and verticality is extreme, isn't it? It's manifested in every single painting.

Although not evident in quite every painting of course, horizontality and verticality do come to dominate the coordinates of Scully's work from a very early stage. If one were to try to pinpoint when the x- and y-axes against which Scully's imagination would rotate for decades definitively established themselves – the turning point when perpendicularity prevailed as the principal grammar of his visual language – 1969 emerges as perhaps the most pivotal moment in his development. In his second year at Newcastle University, Scully found himself absorbing a rich array of aesthetic influences, from the precision of Op artists such as Bridget Riley to the existential rawness of Samuel Beckett's play *Waiting for Godot*, with which he connected deeply after attending a student performance. But it was a trip to Morocco during the same year that awakened something in Scully's soul and left the most profound impression on him.

kg What took you to Morocco?

ss That's a very interesting question. I was in Newcastle fixing up this Ford van, and I got a group of students together and went to Morocco very purposefully because I just thought it would have to be visually incredible. And it was. It had a dramatic and lasting effect on me. Of course I was following in the footsteps of Matisse, who was my great hero.

Scully's admiration for Henri Matisse was passionate. He would go on to write his thesis at Newcastle on Matisse's *The Dance* (1910). In particular, Scully was fascinated by Matisse's ability to translate the cadences of motion into the stasis of paint. 'In truth the major goal of my art', Scully wrote in an article for *American*

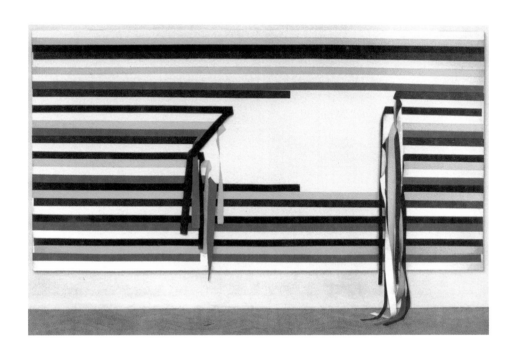

Morocco, 1969

The Moroccan, 1982

Art in 2003, recalling the hold that Matisse had on him 'is that play between rhythm, the inner rhythm of things, and ideas... Art is not really a question of conclusions or closed opinion. It is something that keeps us alive, and it becomes more vital as the world continues on its merry slide.' By 'following in the footsteps of Matisse', Scully wasn't just engaged in academic research. This was a spiritual quest.

ss I remember driving down through Spain, moving south, and stopping in Seville. As you drive through Spain, you become more aware of Morocco because of the ceramic art everywhere – in the streets, in the street signs – and also the beautiful metalwork in the windows that you find in many Spanish towns. The further south you go, the stronger it gets.

You know the pasodoble always seemed, in a way, like a fusion of European and Moroccan influences, and this was very attractive to me – the sense of controlled emotion. It goes back to what we were talking about earlier: it has always been very deep in me, that sense of highly structured emotion. You have it in Spanish culture, in the dancing and the castanets and the rhythm. It's very different from, let's say, the waltz, which comes from Germany.

As we went south, I found the landscape and the light more and more attractive. We would be on campsites, interacting with the Moroccan people, and it was fantastic. The heat was incredible. I remember the heat was something that I adored. It was so hot that we had to drive at night because the van kept overheating in the day. And the visuals were making me kind of crazy. You know, all the tents on the beach. I got right into it.

I've told the story before about Muhammad and how he gave me his djellaba. I gave him some cigarettes and let him drive my van, which he nearly destroyed. This Moroccan boy, you know, he was my age. We became friends and he spoke

English quite well, I must say. We made fish on a campfire. We were very close to the ground all the time.

I'll never forget the little Jack Russell dog. I saw a little dog go under a car and come spinning out the back. It was short enough to have been merely injured. So I pulled up the car and there was an old man tormenting this little dog. It was taking refuge in a scrawny bush. I managed to pick up the dog and brought it into the van. This adorable little dog sat on my lap as I drove all around Morocco for about six weeks. It was an extraordinary little dog. We would go around looking for a home for it because of the quarantine laws in England. I drove everybody crazy with this dog and people said to me, 'How come you love this dog so much that we have to go riding around everywhere looking for a home for it?' They were getting really angry with me. In the end, we found a beautiful place in Casablanca that was a dog's paradise. It had swings and slides, and I left the little dog there, where it would be looked after. I loved that dog so much, but I couldn't bring it back to England.

What Scully did bring back to England was an ignited imagination, its very circuitry all but overridden by the rhythms of Moroccan art. 'After visiting Morocco,' Scully would later recall, 'I became fascinated by cloth, by pattern, and by the way pattern moved as it was carried around by the people... The cloth... is absorbent. The light falls into it... The people of Morocco wrap themselves in this cloth when they are seated. And every time it's different. When they walk the material and the stripes move rhythmically with them, creating a slow dance that reflects the human inside it and the light, wind and air around.' More than anything, what left the most indelible mark on Scully's mind was the inexhaustible potential of the stripe – how verticality and horizontality could hardwire his creativity. 'In Morocco,' he told an interviewer in 2014, 'I saw these stripes everywhere. It was fascinating to me because the stripes were connected, not

Sean drawing on the beach, Essaouira, Morocco, 1996

Mexico Malloy, 1983
Mexico Christmas Day, 1983

to the idea of order, but to the hypnotic idea of rhythm, and to music. It really affected me, because I'm a very musical person, I come from a musical family.'

Almost immediately, Scully's work began to vibrate with that profound influence. At first, the perpendicularly orientated stripes that have come to define the artist's work were deployed as a unique visual dialect that blended accents of European Op Art and American minimalism. During the 1970s, this inimitable admixture gave way to a more thoroughgoing minimalist endeavour as Scully pursued the movement's possibilities as far as they could go. Although, ultimately, he grew weary of minimalism's austerities and rigorous eviction of the human, he never lost patience with the stripe itself – the endlessly resilient and reinventable symbol with which he had fallen in love in Morocco. Though the stripe had, in a sense, led him to minimalism, he knew it could lead him back out again. He just needed a catalyst: a fresh flint to strike against the stoniness of minimalism and inflame the stripe anew. He needed to take another trip.

KG   Morocco, of course, wasn't the only 'otherwhere' to ignite your imagination. You would later visit Mexico and it would have a profound impact too. Mexico seems to have been crucial to your accessing the full meaning and potential of your earlier trips to North Africa.

SS   Yeah, that's a very good reading. I had already had the experience in Morocco. In a sense, physically, the two countries are very similar because they're the same colour. They're the colour of sand and dust, of dried-out sandy dirt. When I went to Mexico in 1980, I had actually wanted to go to Cartagena. I was very exhausted by New York, as was Catherine [Lee, the artist, and Scully's then-wife]. I remember she was close to tears with the fatigue of it. It is such an exhausting city if you're a young embattled artist. I remember we had put down a deposit for a vacation in Cartagena that got cancelled.

I went to the Union office in Princeton and asked if I could borrow $2,000, and when they said 'sure' I nearly fell over. We had the money for a vacation and we both needed it incredibly. We were emptied out by the city and by the struggle. So instead [of Cartagena] we went to Mexico.

I remember looking for somewhere else to go and I saw this place called Ixtapa. I just liked the way it sounded. So I said, 'Let's go there.' On the way, we stopped off in Mexico City. In the hotel there was a card about a trip to see the pyramids at Teotihuacan – I didn't know anything about this stuff. It was organized by a Canadian expat and he had a big American car. He took us and two American ladies out to Teotihuacan. That started my absolute love affair with Mexico because, you see, it's not beautiful vistas that I look for, it's cultural significance, cultural profundity. I'm always curious. Why is it like this? Why does that look like that? Why was that built like that? And then there are the Olmec, Toltec and Aztec [civilizations]. I know about all this stuff now. We went to the museum of archaeology and it blew my mind. You saw these wonderful things. It was like going to Egypt in Latin America.

Then I became very encouraged. We found ourselves in a hotel designed by a disciple of Luis Barragán [a celebrated Mexican architect in whose Cuadra San Cristóbal, a modernist masterpiece on the outskirts of Mexico City, Scully was invited to show in 2018]. Those circles are always being completed in my life. The hotel was beautifully designed, very minimal. It was like a beehive. It was as if you'd put boxes together in a grid and then sliced them at just the right angle to provide every cubicle with its own courtyard and an ocean view.

We discovered this little town, Zihuatanejo, and we used to go back there all the time. That's where I did my seminal watercolour, which was called *Wall of Light*; I just wrote 'wall of light' under it. I painted it on the beach with my

Sean Scully 3.25.85#1

3.25.85 #1, 1985

Wall of Light 4.84, 1984

little watercolour set. We would make these trips around in a rented car, finding all the pyramids. The light would change amazingly in ways that you wouldn't imagine. The colours on the stones would be incredible. The light there is very harsh, and the nights are extremely dark.

KG You mention the stones and the light on the ruins. When I look at your work, especially the work created after your trips to Mexico, what strikes me is the sense of fragmentation and incompleteness. There is an undercurrent of ruin at play. For me, the 'Wall of Light' series always calls to mind the spirit of Wordsworth's 'Ruined Cottage', say, or the fragmented structure of his poem 'Tintern Abbey' – a hefty materiality that is 'far more deeply interfused', as Wordsworth says.

Scully responds to my question with a promising 'yeah' before having to put the conversation temporarily on hold. I am keen to hear him reflect more on notions of ruin in his work, but when he returns his mind, perhaps fittingly, has moved on from thoughts of fragmentation and incompleteness, and my question is left hanging there. He is eager to share, instead, an incident that he has just recalled from one of his many visits to Mexico. It proves to be an amusing digression.

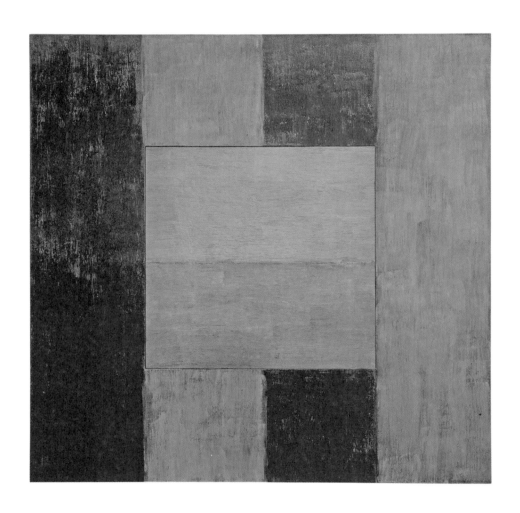

Breath, 1987–90

CHAPTER EIGHT

Hammering

ss I'm driving down in Mexico and we get stopped every time we nearly break a red light. And it's $20, you know. You do the double, triple handshake because after you've just been ripped off by this cop then you're brothers. I drive into Puerto Vallarta. In my usual Sean Scully reckless fashion, I'd forgotten my driver's licence in New York, but I decided that I would just drive around anyway, because I'm a fairly informal fellow, particularly where the law is concerned. So I'm sitting in the car, and a guy comes up to me and tells me I can't park there, and of course he wants $20. By this time I'd had enough of it, because I'd already paid off a couple of guys for nearly breaking the traffic lights. So I say to this guy, 'I'm not giving you anything.' He says to me, 'Okay, give me your driver's licence.' The whole conversation took place in English because I wouldn't give him any Spanish. I wanted him to be at a disadvantage.

What I did next amazed even me, and I've done some fairly lawless things in my day. I pull out Catherine Lee's driver's licence with her picture on it, and I can assure you she doesn't look anything like me. I give the driver's licence to this guy, and he's looking at the licence and me, back and forth, trying to make these two images overlap. He says, 'Is this your driver's licence?' And I just look him straight in the eyes and say 'yes'. Then he starts doing the same thing again, looking left then right, left then right, trying to resolve this conundrum. He asks me if my family name is 'Catherine', like my name was 'Lee Catherine', and I say 'yes' with such certainty that the visual information that entirely contra-dicted what I was saying was undone.

This, in a way, demonstrated to me why we have conceptual art. It's asking you not to believe your own eyes. What it's saying is: this is something that really it's not. It's making visual claims for authenticity that's just informational but isn't borne out by what you see. It's so fascinating – the psychology of it overpowered the evidence. In the end, he wrote me a parking ticket and went on his grumpy way. But that's Mexico. There's a lot of topsy-turvy energy there.

There is one manifestation of the 'topsy-turvy energy' generated by Mexico that pulsed through Scully's imagination that I have been meaning to ask him about for years. Or rather, ask him about again. I wonder if he'll remember this. Some years back, in 2011, the day after my wife, Sinéad, and I got engaged, she, Sean, and I went out to celebrate at a restaurant by the sea in Barceloneta. Eventually, conversation turned to the book that I was writing at the time, *100 Works of Art That Will Define Our Age*, which dared to predict which works of contemporary art would be remembered by posterity. I mentioned to Scully that I was going to include one of his paintings in my selection. I already had one in mind, but I was curious which work he himself might have chosen. There was only one rule: it had to be something created after 1989, the book's starting point. I asked Scully if he recalled the conversation.

KG Do you remember which work you proposed?

SS I don't.

KG Your 1990 painting *Durango*.

SS That's very interesting.

KG Yes, but before you could explain why you would pick *Durango*, you got a call and had to leave rather urgently. Since then, we have never returned to that subject but I am still fascinated.

Durango is not one of the paintings that you tend to discuss a great deal, or to which you attach many anecdotes in your lectures and talks. When you have mentioned it in passing, you've described it as a 'threatening' painting that represents a pretty dark vision. So I've always wanted to know, what is it about *Durango*?

ss Well, let me start off with the title. Durango is a very harsh state in Mexico. It has beautiful parts, no question, and it has some very interesting valleys, but it also has a lot of high places that are arid. It's difficult to eke out a living there agriculturally. There's a lot of stone in Durango. I've driven through it, over the Sierra Madre at night with no head-lights. So I know the northern part of Mexico very well and it's not for tourists, let's say. The painting also reminds me of poems by T. S. Eliot, 'The Waste Land' and 'The Hollow Men'. There's something relentlessly harsh about Durango, and there's something relentlessly harsh about the poems too, and I'm sure he's right that that's how the world will end – with a 'whimper', not a 'bang'. There is that quality in the painting in its symmetrical asymmetry or its asymmetrical symmetry, whichever way you'd like to put it. It's a painting that wants to unify but is, in a sense, broken. It's an insupportable way of working, long term, making paintings in that way. I don't know any artist who could literally keep that up or would want to. It is a threatening painting.

I remember painting it on Duane Street [New York] in my studio loft where it only just fit. I made it on a wooden ladder, running up and down the ladder. It took an extraordinary physical commitment. Also, I have to say, to touch once again on a very painful subject, that the death of Paul was very unresolved during this period.

In 1983, Scully's son, Paul, was killed in a car accident in London. He was 18, only a year younger than Scully was when Paul was

Durango, 1990

Hammering, 1990

TRIPTYCH

TO BE WITH
WEST OF WEST

Neither of these paintings allude to the
sacred, they refer to something more important,
more contemporary, which is human
relationship. How to handle, how to live with
relationship, and how to be. This is our
central problem now. And temporarily more
urgent than the issue of God or Godot.

Sean Scully. Germany. July 5. 2008.

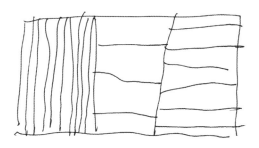

Handwritten page, 'Triptych', 2008

born. The tragedy would change Scully and his art forever. For a period of time, all vibrancy of colour was siphoned from the surface of his work. On more than one occasion, reflecting on this difficult time, Scully has told me how he 'lost his mind'.

ss Paul's death provoked many dark paintings – fierce paintings, I would say – because there's nothing like a geometric rage. That is the most angry of all, I believe, because it's strapped in and seething. There is something very dark and brooding about the painting that scares other paintings away from it.

KG It's a triptych...

ss It's divided into a triptych, and we all know that the triptych has some kind of a reference to either infinity or the sacred. I've used a triptych very often and also in *Durango*'s partner, *Hammering*, and there's another one called *Day Night* [1990], which is a painting I still have that I like very much. It has a kind of narrative to it, a slight sense of changing, as the Post-Impressionists did for example. In *Durango*, there's really very little relief. The triptych, and the bulge in the middle – which gives it even more body, more weight – is constantly disrupting the attempt of the brushstrokes to unify the surface, physically, with its drumming. The surface keeps trying to break down. So in that sense, I suppose, it has something to do with Cubism. Also, the severity of the colour reminds me of some of those Cubist paintings where you've got classicism and unity, but simultaneously you've got the crisis of the object. They are deeply divided paintings: everything in the world is being molested, but they achieve a kind of classicism. I won't say they're ironic, but they're certainly divided, like a two-headed dog. *Durango* has something of that in it. There's a very powerful sense of crisis in that painting, and at the same time a fierce refusal to submit, or a fierce insistence on physically – by application, by

Day Night, 1990

Winter Days, 1990

devotion, by passion, by work – holding something together. That's the way I read that painting.

KG 'Read' is an interesting word. I remember you saying once that your paintings tell stories. Triptychs can be interpreted as having beginnings, middles, and ends. What kind of stories do your paintings tell?

SS The issue I had with abstract painting is that it ended up as a grey square without a title – 'Untitled, 87', you know. So then I decided to reintroduce narrative into it. In the case of *Heart of Darkness*, I was accompanied by a book while I was making the painting. So, as a westerner, I view the paintings, the triptychs, as moving from left to right and then back again from right to left, and giving a sense of travel or change within a painting. With *Heart of Darkness*, the central panel is the most compressed, but also the most grounded in a way. It's referring to the colours of the earth – browns with heavy paint application, very broad bands of colour. It's as if the painting starts out very energetically, emblematically, making reference to African masks, which I had been collecting at that time – particularly Songhai masks, which have these beautiful black and white lines running around them. They were very attractive to me. I striped it up with a lot of underpainting, of course, but with very energetic, arresting colour. Then the colour falls into itself in the middle section; it connects itself to the ground. I was thinking about how to resolve the next panel – the third one. There's that well-known story of me coming along the back of Lispenard Street in Tribeca and seeing the way that the columns were painted. They looked as if they'd been done by somebody who had never painted black and yellow stripes before. I saw these stripes and said, 'Yeah, that's what I need.'

What I was doing really was composing the painting in a sense, musically, because in the symphonic structure

Four Days, 1990

7.5.90, 1990

or in the concerto structure the middle section is usually melancholic or grave. It's usually everybody's favourite, too. In beautiful chamber music you come to the middle movement, the second movement, and it's all sorrow, as in the piano concerto by Rachmaninov. The second movement is tragic, it's heart-rending. So when I was making a lot of those triptychs, I tended to make the middle panel slow and sonorous, and the wings, so to speak, were more energetic. They would lift the painting. That was the idea, that they would provide entry and exit and return. The middle panel was always working as this emotional mediator between the two ends. You can see that in many of them.

You can indeed. Perhaps this sombre mediation occurs most powerfully in the painting that Scully dedicated to the memory of his son. *Paul* is a large triptych that consists of, from left to

I D E A

Moosewach Sept 16 . 06

An idea is more powerful
than an object, Because objects
decay and ideas get repeated.
Why do I make objects? Because
objects decay. And as they decay
they strangely gather more power
in the form of pathos, with paintings
this is especially true. A great
painting seems to gain power as it
ages. It has a strangely interactive
relationship with time! It looks older,
but it looks better. Not like us. But
made by us.

Handwritten page, 'Idea', 2006

Paul, 1984

right: a wide panel (the widest of the three sections) displaying four broad black and white horizontal stripes; a more slender central section that protrudes outwards and bears three narrower grey and black vertical stripes running the height of the work; and a third panel (whose width is in between that of the other two sections) presenting three rich crimson and black vertical stripes that are, respectively, twice as wide as the vertical stripes in the central section. In construction, triptychs were traditionally intended to fold into themselves along hinged seams on either side of the central panel in order to establish, conceptually, a kind of carpentered embrace. Though classical in origin and therefore antedating Christian iconography, the clasping element of the triptych design was nevertheless especially appealing to medieval artists seeking a humane format for depicting the crucifixion and deposition of Christ; it implied, in its very construction, a gathering of the depicted body into the fabric of the work – an entombment within an entombment. The design of Scully's *Paul* at once embraces and poignantly resists the religious rationale of that design. On the one hand, the work's central protrusion suggests a kind of solemn mausoleum for the continued presence of the body that it memorializes. On the other, the materiality of that sepulchre within the work confounds the imagined possibility of ever folding the work shut or completing its embrace. The result is a painting that forever asserts its own bodiliness while, at the same time, lamenting the loss of bodiliness: a work whose insistent physicality steadfastly refuses to concede the finality of final breaths.

I'm conscious, self-conscious even, that the way I describe and respond to Scully's work – as I have here, in words taken from an essay I wrote for the catalogue that accompanied a major retrospective of Scully's work at the National Gallery of Ireland in 2015 – is a critic's response, not an artist's. I'm keen to know how such articulations are received by the artist himself. Is it with interest or bemusement? Gratitude or irritation?

KG What is your reaction to critical writing about you? Do you ever respond to it in the work, or is it something that just floats past you?

SS Oh, I'm very interactive. I'm a very social human being. I also think that, as Socrates famously said, life without criticism has no value. I believe that. You shouldn't just get away with stuff and be adored all the time; and certainly if you make abstract paintings, that won't happen to you in England. It's the reason I had to depart, even though it caused me, I must say, great sorrow. I do love England, and I love the way the people are. In this coronavirus you can see how they hold together and how kind they are to each other, and how a lot of old people have stuff brought to them by neighbours and by decent people living around them. Whereas in America, it's the United States of blame. It's a fundamentally fractured society, and I think it can't come together. It's got a deep fissure in it.

KG Have you seen that fissure deepen in the time that you've been there?

SS Well, I haven't lived in America for a very long time. I've lived in New York, which is not America. I have a very strong relationship with Texas, but Texas is quite unified in a certain sense. The profound issues that separate different points of view in America are so ironclad that I think they are irresolvable, and it probably shouldn't have been united as a country. The sensibilities are so entirely different, and the points of view are so entirely different. This issue of gun control is utterly divisive, as is social welfare, and so on. In my opinion, we have the perfect model for government. It's in Scandinavia. It already exists – a perfect fusion of enterprise, profit, ambition, social conscience, sharing and environmental responsibility.

It isn't long before talk of the fractious nature of American society gives way to a discussion about the fractious nature of that other 'country' of which Scully is an outspoken citizen: contemporary art. We chat for a while about how the unfolding story of art history has changed in recent times, from appearing to adhere to a linear narrative of one movement being replaced by another – medieval by Renaissance, Rococo by Romantic, Impressionism by Post-Impressionism, Cubism by abstract expressionism, etc. – to something more frayed and fragmentary: a multiverse of varying visual voices, each reacting to different pressures and against different ancestors. Scully's friend, the critic Arthur Danto, called it the 'end of art' in the 1980s. But that end, of course, coincided interestingly not with the conclusion, but with the coming to maturity of Sean Scully. I was curious to hear Scully's thoughts on this positioning of him both at the end of art and at the beginning of its afterlife.

ss   You could describe the 1980s as a new wave coming in backwards. You imagine a wave as something that washes into the shore. But this was coming in reverse, and what it was bringing with it was a rejigging of everything and having people like Georg Baselitz painting German Expressionism upside down, or [Anselm] Kiefer making very powerful things that look like operatic stage sets. So you have things that seem more connected with the past than with any kind of future. And the other interesting thing that's happening is that video didn't do what it was going to do.

KG   It keeps trying...

ss   It keeps trying. But here's the big problem with technological dependency: it lives by the sword and it dies by the sword. It cuts a swath when it's brand new, but the edge gets blunt very quickly as it's replaced, and then it looks old. But paintings seem to gain power as they get older. Now that,

Playground, 2015

Ghost Gun, 2016
Ghost Night, 2018

to me, is an extremely interesting point. The *Mona Lisa* has no value because if you tried to buy it you would have to pay the equivalent of a small country. Maybe Ireland. And there it is: this unassuming, enigmatic expression on the face of a woman who's not a starlet, but a nice-looking woman. I think this raises a lot of points about the survival of painting. It doesn't give up its secrets. It has about it something insoluble – inscrutable might be a better word. Great paintings seem to be unconquerable – I've noticed that, since I've been an artist. I've seen lots of people whizz past me and then break down. It's a cruel business, longevity. Unless, of course, you have it. Then it's not so cruel.

KG Do you think this insoluble power is peculiar to painting, over, say, drawing and sculpture?

SS Oh, that's such an interesting question! Let me preface my answer by saying that I'm not proposing that I know the definitive answer. There is a mystery in this subject, which is why it is so captivating, and why it has held me for so long, and why it took me away from my peers when I was a teenager. I was very connected, back then, to vast energy, to hip energy. You know, I was very hip. I was right in and of the moment. But there was something deeper and fascinating about these images. Whether these images are more profound than the sculptures, I don't know. The sculptures that I find most arresting are the ones that don't say much. They just kind of mumble something and then you think, what? Huh? What was that? They withhold as much as they say. That's true also of painting because I don't like [the 15th-century Florentine painter Paolo] Uccello as much as I like other artists. The things that seem to touch people and endure are the things that say less. They're things that you can't really explain. They say enough, but they don't say everything. This is registered perfectly, as a metaphor, in the smile of the *Mona Lisa*. That smile isn't laughter, and it isn't passion. It isn't ironic, and it isn't irritated. It's something that's in between everything. She keeps looking, smiling that very faint smile that holds a lot back. It's very regal in some ways, though there's no great sense of social rank – except, of course, she can fork out to have some guy paint her. I mean, back then he wasn't Leonardo yet. So there's this painting that is warm but not hot, that implies but doesn't state, and it's holding back an enormous amount. It's as if there was a wave but the wave is frozen; you can feel that you can't see everything that it's holding. It probably has something to do with the way we love how whales speak. We love it because we can't understand what they're saying. If we knew they were saying things like 'Get out the way', we probably wouldn't like it so much. But it has so much mystery in it. It's old and it's contemporary.

CHAPTER NINE

Between You and Me

ss My relationship with Oisin has had a profound effect on my
    psychological condition...

It's 20 May 2020, and Scully and I are talking and recording again.
Lockdown was declared almost exactly two months ago in the
United States, where he is, and in Ireland, where I am. There's
a reverse symmetry to our situations (he lives in my native land,
and I in his) that perhaps helps us to appreciate the other's perspective and sense of exile. Our immediate families are mirrors
too. We're both isolating with our wives and our only sons. Our
devotion to our children – Scully to Oisin, I to Caspar – is absolute and very often the chief topic of our conversations. Our
respective email inboxes and WhatsApp accounts are brimming
with photographic evidence of obsessive fatherly pride. Here's
Oisin leaping with an umbrella. Here's Caspar holding a crayon.
In a prose statement composed by Scully in 2010, when Oisin was
a year old, he tenderly chronicles an affectionate routine he and
his son used to undertake in his studio.

  'Every morning Oisin, my fourteen-month-old son, and I
walk hand-in-hand through the studio,' Scully wrote. 'His little hand in mine is at just the right height to make it pleasant
for both of us. The studio is cavernous. Seven meters high,
ten meters wide, and twenty long. Against the long walls the
big paintings of mine stand leaning. Oisin and I pass by them
together, and he usually likes to stop to kiss them, which we call
"kissing the paintings". I call it "kissing the paintings", and Oisin
nods his approval. Then he commences to dutifully lurch against
each one, and plant a sincere kiss on it. He befriended the color
black slowly, which is understandable, since he is so connected

Oisin Scully within a painting, 2011

Eleuthera, 2017

to the urgency of his unfolding life and regret is in a possible distant future. However, he came around to it.' But just as Oisin came around to black in his father's work, Scully himself began coming around to the warmth of bright colour, which had been largely absent from his painting. The return of colour is a topic I'm keen to explore a little further.

KG There's a lot more joy in your colouration since Oisin arrived.

SS Yeah, more than there was when I painted *Durango*. When I painted *Durango*, I think my life, emotionally, could not have been bleaker. The same is true of a lot of other paintings too, like *Between You and Me*. *Between You and Me* is a painting that I'm very fond of. It has within it a painting that turns around in a circle that goes nowhere. Like the Rudyard Kipling story of the tiger that chases itself around a tree, this painting goes around in circles and it's encased in a thick wooden frame, set within a big painting...

KG ...which is very unusual for one of your works – to have a framed canvas inside an otherwise frameless work. And then there's a second, slightly larger, inset within that same painting, one which is not framed by wood. So two smaller canvases embedded into one larger canvas...

SS Yeah, it's a unique painting. I have made paintings where one inset is encased in metal, which can work as framing, which is a form of protection, or as incarceration, which is a form of isolation. A painting that I think could be very interesting to discuss in relation to *Between You and Me* is another one I'm extremely fond of – *Spirit*, which is in the Reina Sofia in Madrid. It's a black and white painting where two insets are encased in metal. This suggests, of course, a relationship with Arte Povera, which there is in my work, in the sculpture. The earliest sculpture I made was an old mattress that was

Between You and Me, 1988

Spirit, 1992

sprayed and then hung as a readymade. *Between You and Me* is interesting to me because it has got one inset on the right side, which is in a sea of paint; it's part of the sea of paint. Then the inset that's framed, it's framed in a kind of rough wood and it's left, somehow, spinning its own endless story and isolation – both in the painting and isolated from the painting.

KG Elsewhere in your work, when you use wood as a support, it's usually salvaged from a place of personal significance. Do you remember where the wood to frame this inset came from?

SS Oh yeah, it was salvaged from Duane Street where I had my studio in the loft of an old textile warehouse. When I acquired the loft, I had access to a lot of free wood. That loft was an endless source of wood. You can see that it's not fancy wood at all. And the paintings *Long Night* and *Round and Round*: I painted those on wooden boards that were left. What's so fascinating is that many years later a very young art critic from Belfast wrote about my work and referred to bodies hidden under floorboards, and I had actually painted those two paintings on some discarded floorboards!

Scully is recalling the review I wrote of a retrospective of his work, 'Constantinople, or the Sensual Concealed', which opened at the Ulster Museum in late 2009 – the gig that sparked our wonderful friendship. 'Midway through the nine galleries and sixty paintings which comprise "Constantinople, or the Sensual Concealed" – a thought-provoking retrospective of Sean Scully's work,' so I wrote in the *Times Literary Supplement* in January 2010, 'visitors are confronted by a larger-than-life photographic fresco of the artist in action. Splattered in pigment, Scully scowls at us with irritated intensity, like someone interrupted burying bodies under floorboards. For thirty-five years, he has built a reputation

Long Night, 1985

Round and Round, 1985

on repetition – enormous canvases of cramped, abutting stripes, which refuse to confess connection to any living thing. Yet beneath the shouldered planks of filthy ochres, slate clays and scabbing reds stirs an unexpected warmth of vision which aligns the works more to the humid golds of Byzantine icons than to Rothko's vaporous saturations, more to the muscular light of Turner than to the frenetic flinging of Jackson Pollock.'

KG How have those floorboards that you repurposed held up in the works in which they were incorporated? Have they stood the test of time?

SS Very well. Of course, medieval artists were painting on wood, and this brings up the issue of the painting being a thing. It's not an image. The wood confuses this notion of sign or symbol or image. Because you get pushed, by the materiality of it, into the question 'What is it?' Instead of being in the interpretive room, you get shoved into the reality room. What is this thing? Is it a painting or is it a thing?

KG Yeah, it's not an image of a thing, it's the thing itself. These boards, these materials, which transformed these paintings from images or signs into things, eventually disappear from your work. Why is that? Is it because the wood and boards you did use had an important personal backstory, and when you ran out you couldn't just replenish wood that had meaning?

SS Exactly as you've said it. Because it is, in a way, Arte Povera, poor art. It is bound up with the invisible mythology of Duane Street. I'm very attached to these old things. In the bedroom where I am now, for example, there's a Mongolian wardrobe that I bought in Chelsea. It wasn't very expensive but it's from Mongolia. It was obviously a bridal present for two young people. It has a picture of paradise on the doors

Liliane, 2010

Oisin's Breath, 2010

and all these mythological animals protecting paradise, and dragons that would guard the gates of paradise. These things become incredibly important to me. This chair, for example, that belonged to Charles Choset. Every day I sit on this chair and I touch where he touched. And I have things from my childhood that I hold on to. So all these objects that I've had through my life are incredibly important to me. They get so much emotional patina on them that I can't ever let them go.

KG They've absorbed an aspect of you...

SS I cleaned all those boards. I recycled them by incorporating them into my work, which I think is so very important not only for the environment, but for the history of that wood. Trees give us everything. These boards had an emotional relationship to me. When I first got the studio on Duane Street I was working with my friend Nick, who was over from London. He was a close friend of Peter Nadin, who is a very dear friend of mine and a well-known artist in New York. Peter and Nick helped me. So we did the whole loft together – 5,000 square feet – and organized a dumpster.

In those days, everything was a lot rougher. When you organized a dumpster in New York back in the '70s, everybody and their uncle would fill it up for you if you took your eyes off it for half a minute. We had to make sure that we got all the junk out of the loft before the rest of the world filled the dumpster, because we only had enough money for one. You know, I was nearly broke fixing this loft up. So we opened the window on the second floor, and we were throwing stuff out the window into the dumpster. This was outrageously illegal, and dangerous, of course. We were running around trying to get everything organized, and I heard a sound so strange that I couldn't quite identify what it was until I looked down at my shoe and saw a nail sticking up through my foot. It had been hammered into one of those very boards that we are talking about – the boards that are now in my paintings. It had gone straight through my shoe, into my foot and out the other side. Nick and I had to decide what we were going to do. I was harpooned, stuck on this board.

We devised a strategy for how we were going to remove this board. I wasn't going to just step off it because we were both afraid that I would pass out. Nick was wonderful about this. He followed me faithfully with this board so that it didn't stress my foot. We would practise counting to three – one, two, three – and after a few goes we said, 'Okay, this is it! No more dress rehearsals. One, two, three!' and he pulled the board and the nail out of my foot as fast as he could. Of course, we couldn't afford to stop working because of the damn dumpster. I put my sock back on and went back to work. I woke up the following morning and I saw a strange object at the end of the bed, which I recognized as a melon but it was actually my foot with some toes on it. So I hobbled up to St Vincent's Hospital. I didn't have to wait very long when they saw the size of my foot. This guy said to me, 'You could have been dead by now.' When I decided to come to New York, I wasn't messing around.

KG Wow, art nearly crucified you.

CHAPTER TEN

Language of Light

Scully and I are talking about artists who criticize other artists, and whether such attempts to shape the cultural climate in which one lives and works are ever effective. Or wise...

ss It's a little bit like walking around a forest and criticizing the trees. You know, saying this tree shouldn't be here or that's a bad tree. That tree isn't as good as this tree. All the trees in the forest are fighting for light in the same way that artists are fighting for light. In the art world, there's really no difference. You're in a habitat and you're a living creature and you're doing the best you can for yourself. It's not necessary to try and rearrange the pieces as if they were static pieces on a board.

I think of the art world as a kind of natural, moving, swaying, drifting current of work, humanity and enterprise. I don't really think I can organize it very much. What I tend to do is be interested in things that I feed off. If I see something I want, I probably would take it. And why not? I expect the same treatment from others. But judging other artists, putting other artists down, is a very bad idea.

KG Putting out bad mojo isn't really good for the soul anyway, is it?

ss No, it's always better to be generous. Jealousy is very destructive, as is competitiveness. When you make art, you have to be expansive. You're breathing out, and you're allowing your intellect to create and think of ideas – to be as open and ebullient as it can be, to your maximum capacity, whatever

paintings speak with the
language of light. Silent with
an inner light. An outer light which
is the image and an inner light which
is the soul.

Handwritten page, 'Language of Light', 2000

that is. If you are resentful of somebody else, and if you are jealous and competitive, I really believe that your spirit and your imagination shrink exponentially. You can't create like that. You have to create with largesse. As Bob Dylan says, don't get me down in the hole that you're in.

Scully is echoing a line from Dylan's hypnotic song 'It's Alright Ma (I'm Only Bleeding)', from the album *Bringing It All Back Home* (1965). Dylan imagines a petty figure with a flaming tongue, twisted by society and filled with resentment, who drags others down into the ditch he's in. Scully and I share a deep love of Dylan and often allow allusion to his lyrics to serve as shared shorthand for the points we are making. Over the course of our ongoing conversations, Dylan, it so happens, was busy releasing singles from his new album, *Rough and Rowdy Ways*. In one song Dylan released around that time, he echoes Walt Whitman's self-assessment of his own inner vastness in the song's eponymous line 'I contain multitudes' – a phrase, it struck me, that could likewise serve as an epigraph to the breadth of Scully's reminiscences and views.

ss You have to meet somebody's work with love. Art, or creativity, is ultimately a question of love.

kg I agree, but not everyone would. Harold Bloom famously argued that the whole history of literature is a succession of fierce frictions and Oedipal tensions – Milton doing battle with Shakespeare, Wordsworth at war with Milton, etc. Each generation, Bloom thought, misreads its ancestors and in doing so opens up a space in which to operate. It isn't love but an 'anxiety of influence' – a deep fear that everything's already been said – that drives creation. Do you ever feel a competitiveness with your forebears?

ss You have these forebears, that's true, and you have to meet them and join them in some way. You're competing, of course, with history. You're competing with what's been done before, but you can only do it with a sense of largesse. I was often compared with Rothko because the colour in my work is a little bit reduced and the edges are soft, but the dissimilarities are tremendous. There's a much greater sense of invention – formal invention – in my work. It's significantly more physical. My paintings are more aggressive in their structures. I'm closer, in that sense, to Mondrian. But you're going to bump into somebody no matter which way you go.

I have proceeded, I think, by devouring influences. A great many. I remember one American painter who had an enormous chip on his shoulder. The chip on his shoulder was nearly as big as his entire shoulder, and he used to say he had only one influence: Mondrian. Well, I think that's fatal to only have one influence. That's absurd. I've got fifty influences for sure. I look at them with enormous affection. Now, of course I'm capable of great aggression. You know, I'm a fighter, literally – I kickbox – so I know what it is to compete. At the same time, when you're fighting with a friend, there's also great love there. This is what people don't really understand about boxing. There's a huge amount of love in it. You see the boxers embrace at the end of the fight after they've worked something out. As a side note, one of the things I love about boxers is this: when they win, they often praise God; when they lose, they always blame themselves, which I find very beautiful. So the best things are given to us, and the worst things are our fault.

KG The other side of indebtedness, of course, is influence and appeal. What is at the heart of your appeal to your audience and to other artists? What do you think are the ingredients of enduring appeal?

SS Well, of course, this changes from age to age. I always thought that [the 18th-century French painter Jean-Antoine] Watteau was an extraordinary artist. I think what is so attractive about his work is really the opposite of what is so attractive about Rubens. There's no way to predict what is going to work and what is not going to work. I don't think you can do it with strategy. You have to think with the heart. Ultimately, what people need from art is something emotional. That, I would say, is fundamental. Watteau's paintings are small and they celebrate opulence. He paints pictures of all these aristos on these lovely little islands. But he also intimates that this is a situation that's not going to last. There's a regretful melancholia in the colour of his work, which I have taken somewhat to heart. That's one of my influences. There's a dark joyfulness in his paintings. This touches the heart because you feel such empathy for those people. You see them, in a way, as a little bit silly because there they are rowing out to a kind of pointless party destination. But you also feel sorrow for them because you know that they are doomed. In terms of lifestyle, it's not sustainable. That pointless merry-go-round of opulence is not going to be supported by the people.

I think there has to be something in art that touches the heart. Rembrandt is the great exemplar of this. He's almost everybody's favourite artist, and it's because he shows you something that is, on the one hand, fabulously painted, but on the other truthfully mortal. I think in some ways – and this is not really something I can influence one way or the other because your sense of colour is like your singing voice, it comes out of your spirit – there's a sense of melancholia, or regret, in the colour I use that touches the people that it touches. Obviously it pisses people off who are more Pop.

KG You and Rembrandt are both drawn to very bruised colour, world-weary colour. You also share a kind of majestic vulnerability...

Jean-Antoine Watteau,
Pilgrimage to the Isle of Cythera, 1717

Rembrandt, *Man in a Turban*, 1632

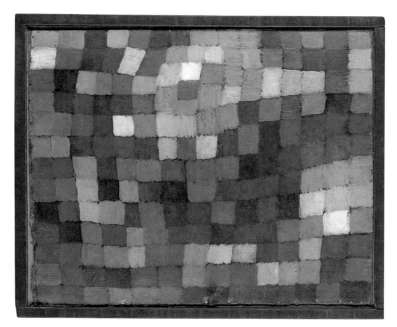

Paul Klee, *May Picture*, 1925

ss Majestic vulnerability! Good God, you're running away with the whole show. That's very beautiful. But I think that nobility is part of it too. A work can't be simply pathetic. Nobody's interested in that. That doesn't hold anybody's attention. The sense of nobility and vulnerability in Rembrandt is extremely moving. He loved. You can see that he loved.

kg His subjects also seem to inhabit a place that is both eternal and dreamlike, and at the same time utterly real. Rembrandt's robes are very otherworldly, yet incontestably tactile. Maybe we could talk for a moment about your own sequence of paintings called 'Robes'. I've always thought they share a certain quality with Paul Klee's grids, which are also dreamlike and cerebral, while at the same time calibrated to the battered colours and geometries of the palpable world.

ss Yeah, that is very interesting. When I was young, before I
     went to art school, I bought one of those Thames & Hudson
     books, *World of Art*, and it was the book on Paul Klee. In fact,
     I bought many of those books. That's how I educated myself.
     I read all those books. I simply fell in love with the abstract-
     ness and the figuration of Klee – the way his subjects would
     drift in and out of figuration. I loved that painting of Sinbad
     in the boat. He did some strange faces and strange animals.
     But he also did these grids. He was very fond of the chequer-
     board. My 'Robe' paintings relate very strongly to my interest
     in Klee. The idea for my 'Robe' paintings comes from the
     Book of Durrow [a 1,300-year-old illuminated manuscript that
     takes its name from a monastery in Durrow, County Offaly,
     Ireland]. There's also an early painting of mine called *Boris
     and Gleb* that is a homage to one of the pages in the *Book
     of Durrow*.

There was one illustration in particular that caught Scully's eye:
a stylized portrait of St Matthew the Evangelist. Characterized
throughout by an intricacy of interlocking, insular lines, the
Book of Durrow devotes an entire page to Matthew, cloaking
him uniquely from chin to ankles in a long robe whose overall
chequerboard design is interrupted by square patches of a con-
trasting criss-cross pattern. At first glance, the post-minimalist
garment does indeed look like it could have been dreamt up by
Scully himself.

ss I was thinking about the cloth, and how robes and materi-
     als have a kind of ceremonial purpose or a magic purpose,
     like the way witch doctors dress up in certain robes. Even
     our doctors today dress up in doctors' coats. It gives them
     a certain authority. That's where I got the title 'Robe' from.
     All those chequerboard paintings I usually call 'Robe'. They
     have a great deal to do with a sense of materiality. The way
     they're painted is very material and illuminated in some way.

St Matthew, from the *Book of Durrow* (MS. 57, fol. 21v), *c.* 650–700,
Library of Trinity College Dublin

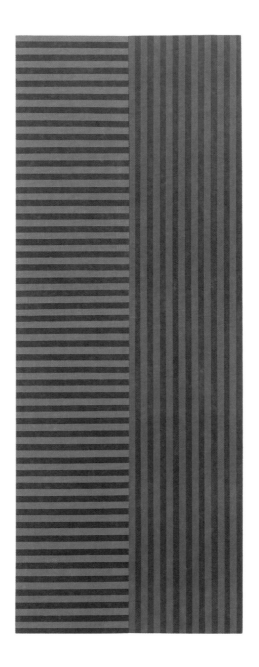

Boris and Gleb, 1980

The surface of the painting and the surface of the material somehow come together in this third reality. They make a conspiration. They conspire to make another fiction. That's what I was trying to do with these paintings. I loved these grids that weren't regular, that swayed and also had a sense of body in them – in the way the Klees do. I was much more interested in the humanism and the off-kilter aspect and the musicality of Klee than I was in a simple kind of minimalism. Here's an interesting thing: Klee played a violin every day. So musicality in Klee is a real thing. It's embedded into the spirit of the work, and it is in my work too because of my musical upbringing. I think that the slightly uneven and hand-drawn quality of these 'Robes' gives them a rhythm, and it gives them a relationship to tapestry or clothing, which of course I've been very interested in since Morocco. I've always thought of them as having a magic quality or a kind of spiritual or musical quality.

One could say that our culture is made by robes. It's made by various ceremonies that we carry out, and that's what positions us in the calendar year. It gives us a sense of occasion, a sense of rank – all kinds of differences are articulated by robes. I'm not just talking about luxury, but the 'Robe' paintings do have a sense of opulence about them because of the way the overpainting allows the underpainting to kind of subvert what's on top of it. This makes a kind of linear drawing that runs through the divisions. This sets up another sub-rhythm.

KG The 'Robe' paintings seem to sew together a materiality and an immateriality of being. You seem lovingly to bestow these robes on subjects of intense affection: your son Paul, for instance, or influences such as Titian. It's as though you've created some sort of ritualistic order in which they are all enshrined, and they've all been issued their ceremonial robes.

Paul's Robe, 2004

Alberto's Robe, 2004

Yellow Robe 8.1.06, 2006

Robe 3.26.08, 2008

Robe 4.1.19, 2019

Titian's Robe Pink
As in the 'Pope' paintings of Titian, I wanted to express something about how we assign transformative power to sacred and ceremonial ROBES. The repeated pattern of the painting is set in opposition and dialogue with the romance of its' painting. It is painted on metal, and the divisions within the painting, as caused by the joints between the metal panels, gives the painting a contemporary materiality. A sense of the Now. Yet the painting, the way the banality of the grid is painted into place = clearly makes a strong reference to romantic painting, with its soft edges and subtle colors. So it's really, a giant ROBE, as an abstracted reality, set free from the figure = to make its own independent relationship with us and its' environment. I see it as luxurious and austere.

Sean Scully 30 Aug 09

Handwritten page, 'Titian's Robe Pink', 2009

Titian's Robe Pink 08, 2008

Titian, *Portrait of Pope Paul III*, c. 1543

ss I love Titian. And you know, he lived long, like me. Titian painted a portrait of Pope Paul III, right? I went to see it. When you see this painting, what you're looking at is, in a sense, the emotion of rank, if I can say it like that. I mean, it would be easier to say that the status of rank is enforced and made by the wearing of the robe. You see that the painting is 80% about the robe – about the clothing. It's fascinating that the materiality of life, the skin of life, is its matter, in a certain sense, its way of surviving. It's the way of ordering. It's the way of making society the skin of things. And there's an incredible painting by him in the Alte Pinakothek in Munich, a mocking of Christ. Again, you see the subject is the skin. It's a brutal, physical painting with these dark red, brownie colours, and you can see its influence on me very easily. I make many paintings that are informed by a kind of heavily painted dark red that has a really strong relationship to Titian.

Because of the Other

ss I don't know if you ever saw that film *Zardoz* [1974] with Sean
Connery opposite a very beautiful English actress, Charlotte
Rampling? They represented human virility, and the whole
world lived inside a bubble. Most people didn't know, and
those who did kept it a secret that they were living inside
a bubble. It was a very rarefied atmosphere because man
had destroyed the environment. They were living in a world
where passion, belief, love and attraction were all strangely
alien because mankind had become a huge society of rarefied irony.

The film was a warning against this, and it always struck
me as a very important message. Not that the technology
in the film was equal to its ambition in those days, but the
message was clear: that we couldn't give up on the things
that make us so vital – that we live, and we fall in love, and
we travel, and we hold things, and we grow old and we die,
and new people come. All this is regenerative. That was the
message of the film.

The 1970s was a period of great irony, and it followed a
headache in the 1960s. These periods of irony always follow
a headache. The '60s were hugely celebratory, and so were the
'80s. You might say that people were living in a fool's paradise,
but we're probably always living in a fool's paradise when we
believe in our optimism. In any case, decades of celebration
are often followed by decades of correction and introspection
and, indeed, irony. That's when irony rears its head.

In the 1970s, there was plenty of it. All these very strict
conceptualists came along. And there was I, insisting on the
virility of art – on the primitive necessity of art – and how

Backs and Fronts (detail), 1981

art couldn't evolve technologically, which was its gift to the world. One cold January afternoon in 1982, David Carrier, who has supported me steadfastly, rang on my funky old doorbell in Duane Street and said, 'Hello! My name is David Carrier. I've just seen *Backs and Fronts* at PS1. Could I visit you?' It was very sweet. He said he used to talk about me, and when he mentioned my name people either said 'He's wonderful' or they would become inflamed with rage. There was a kind of primitive roadblock to their ironic progress.

The stultifying effect that irony has on a culture's soul – on its way of thinking, of creating art and comprehending its purpose – is a topic that Scully returns to frequently when we talk. In a brief prose sketch he wrote in 2005, to which he attached a title that is almost as expansive as the memo itself – 'The Crack of Irony That Hides Out Between Disciplines' – he explores how irony serves as a kind of disingenuous shield that absolves those who wield it from ever having to say what they mean, and mean what they say. 'We live in a time of Sophists,' he wrote. 'That is because now it is relatively easy to be an artist, and if you say you're an artist or curator you can say it for quite a long time without having to prove it with art. The Sophists operate within the crack of irony that hides out between disciplines. This allows for discussion of the interesting, whilst simultaneously avoiding the consequences of the consequent. By dabbling in this and that, by avoiding definitions such as painting, drawing, photography [and] sculpture, it is almost possible for a considerable length of time to avoid critical consequence. The strategy, as a form of careerism, is to avoid consequence, or in a sense: capture. But it is only when an artist is captured that the possibility of greatness or intensity is engaged. Then it starts to be something you can recognize.'

As Scully reflected on the roadblocks to progress that irony throws up and his career-long resistance to all things ironic, my mind suddenly shuttled to a shape of his work that seemed to me to embody the directness and honesty, the 'greatness' and 'intensity', of his own imagination: the ongoing 'Wall of Light' series that began in the late 1990s. I had always wanted to know more about how it was that this celebrated group of large-scale oil paintings should emerge fourteen years after he first attached the poetic phrase 'wall of light' to a watercolour that he painted on a beach in Mexico (see p. 156). It was a non sequitur, I know, but I saw my chance and took it.

KG   Can you tell me about the long gap between the watercolour you painted in 1984 and the extensive 'Wall of Light' series of paintings that would eventually ensue? I'm very interested in that incubation of imagination.

SS   That's a good question. It's something I don't understand about myself; I have a very curious sense of time. I can forget things for a decade and I don't realize that the decade has gone by. This happens quite a lot. My wife finds it very amusing that I mix things up – the dates of things – by ten years. For me, it's not a problem. It illustrates that I'm not fundamentally competitive, which I think is a very important subject. Before we embark on the 'Wall of Light' series, I would like to touch on that subject. People think that art – or other endeavours like poetry, what you do – is based on competitiveness. But it's not. It's based on love: the love of something. I'm not in competition with my contemporaries. As you know, I have a very relaxed sense of arrogance that might be partly responsible for that, I don't know. I really don't worry about who's doing what first.

I've had a lot of ideas that other people have lifted, and they're welcome to them. However, it's not simply an idea, it's the development of its possibilities. The source of the idea, its genesis, its deep root, is what will determine how far you can develop it. It's not really just a question of who did what first. Braque invented Analytical Cubism first and he also invented Synthetic Cubism first. As a Cubist, Picasso is certainly equal to him. I mean, as a pure Cubist, because Picasso was Cubist all his life. What I'm basically getting at is that, in New York in particular, there's a tiresome obsession with competitiveness, and I think it is one of the unfortunate elements that ruined New York's primacy, whereas in Germany and also in England there's a much greater allowance and respect between artists.

I remember when I first went to New York, it wasn't like that. We only talked about art. We never talked about market. Now people bellyache about market all the time. I come, as you very well know, from a gypsy campsite in Inchicore and we lived in a 7 × 7 ft room. So if you are complaining to me about only being able to sell a painting for $100,000, which is the price of a house, you can't expect much sympathy from a person like me. And I never thought about art in purely competitive terms. It's always a question of rapture – being in love with this or that or the other, and combining these influences in your own personal cauldron to make something new. That is, I think, part of the reason why I was able to just park 'Wall of Light' for so long, because I wasn't concerned at all that somebody else might have the idea.

And nobody did have the idea. All those years after I made that watercolour, nobody had come up with the idea of making patchwork paintings, which I find very interesting; that you can just put something, so to speak, under the pillow, and in those intervening years nobody will think of the same thing. People started making similar or related paintings, but only afterwards. I could have made those paintings in '84, of course, when I made the watercolour. But I was doing other things. I wasn't ready to make those paintings.

KG When you made the watercolour, can you remember thinking, 'Aha, this is the start of something big.'

Mexico Vallarta 12.83, 1983

3.29.84, 1984

ss If you look at the Mexican watercolours, there's a whole career there. Actually there are several careers within them, and people have made several careers out of them.

KG You've had several careers out of them.

ss There was a whole encyclopedia of ideas there. I was just very open. You know, considering I make geometry, I'm very open. I was responding to influences, and some of the influences were the shacks in Mexico. And some of the influences were big stone walls. The ancient stone walls fascinated me. So I think that 'Wall of Light' was inspired by the big, clumsy, ungainly, geometrically shaped rocks that are put one on top of – and next to – the other in order to make these massive ruins. What attracted me to those structures is their lack of refinement. I believe that refinement is less important than vitality, which is what we talked about earlier, when we talked about irony. Refinement comes with irony, but you have to have something to refine. Raw sugar is better than refined sugar, in terms of your body. So I like to produce, if possible, raw stuff – raw material that other artists can also use.

Those structures that I kept coming across in Mexico really inspired me by their crudeness, their brutal quality, which you see very strongly in the architecture of Luis Barragán. He was a very refined man, but his architecture is quite brutal. It has a lot in common with the ruins of Mexico – Uxmal, Coba, Tulum, Labna, Sayil, Chichen Itza. All these places are very inspiring in their massiveness and in their frankness. It was a response to that, I think, that caused me to make that beautiful little watercolour on the beach in Mexico, which is in the National Gallery in Washington, DC. I greatly regret that, because it should be with me. We have to borrow it every damn time we want it, which is quite a nuisance.

Traveller 2.84, 1984

Mexico 4.5.88, 1988

I had a lot of other things going on at the same time. I was making discordant relationships, I was challenging the rectangle, I was putting things with other things that didn't fit, and I was making strange diptychs and triptychs. If you look through those Mexican watercolours, you can see that I was coming up with lots and lots of ideas every day. Every time I went down to Mexico, I found it very inspiring.

Wall of Light – I gave it a very special title – I thought was very beautiful. I really liked it, but I was kind of busy. And when I returned to it, I was in the most un-Mexican place I could possibly imagine. I was in the same area we had lived in when we came over from Ireland.

KG The Old Kent Road…

SS Right, the shittiest part of London. I was in my studio on Childers Street in Deptford, which is just around the corner from the Old Kent Road and very close to where we used to live when we came over from Ireland, on Penry Street. I'd been coming back to England from New York in the summer to work for years and had been using that studio for almost a decade. There I was working one afternoon on another black and white painting that was going to be like *Hammering* or *Durango*, which were very relentless paintings. They were a strange fusion of minimalism and abstract expressionism. For some reason, which I still don't understand, nor do I particularly care to, I painted one of the corners orange. But we don't have to know why we do these things, right? You just have to be with the muse, and then you do something new and you accept it. Lily [Liliane Tomasko] was there, and she said, 'Why don't you do something on the other end in orange?' So I did, and the painting became black and white and kind of orange. Then I said, 'It's a strange painting because it becomes relational again. I've gone back to making something relational that was teetering on being an

Liliane Tomasko, London, 1995

all-over argument – consistent from top to bottom and from left to right.' She said, 'Yeah, everything is there because of the other.' And I said, 'That's right', and that's the title of the painting: *Because of the Other*. It's a relational painting, and therefore everything is as it is because of the other.

It wasn't long before I thought to myself, 'This is a "Wall of Light" painting. It's a proto-"Wall of Light" painting and it forms a bridge between the "Wall of Light" paintings as they became and the little painting on the beach [from 1984].' And there it is; there's the story.

Once Scully had crossed that bridge, from the memory of that 'moment of inspiration', as he recalled in a lecture in 2005, 'after looking at the ruins there and seeing how the light changed the

Because of the Other, 1997

Wall of Light Pink, 1998

Wall of Light White, 1998

walls from orange, to blue, to black, to pink in the morning', to a place fourteen years later when he was ready to realize that inspiration's potential, there was no stopping him. Since 1998, Scully has created hundreds of works – from small watercolours to large-scale oil paintings, from luminous aquatints to colossal stone sculptures – centred around the tight tapestry of blocks of compressed colour that characterize the inimitable matrix he evocatively christened 'Wall of Light'. Invariably, the works that bear that title feature bundles of single, double or triple bricks crammed perpendicularly, edge-to-edge, forcing friction between the gnashing slabs. And yet, in spite of the repetition of rhythms from work to work, each manages to echo back a unique music that chronicles the time and place and mood of its making.

In a lecture given by Scully at the Phillips Collection in Washington, DC, in 2005, he reminisced about the particular circumstances that gave birth to one of my favourite instalments in the series, *Wall of Light Desert Night* (1999) – a pulsing puzzle of heat and sand that came about after the artist got lost in Las Vegas. 'It is desperate in Las Vegas,' Scully recalled, 'as there is no sense of proportion. It is disorientating and the opposite of everything I do in my work, which is very much about a bodily sense of proportion. And here I was in a floating reality. One minute I was in Egypt, and the next in medieval England. It was a desperate situation, so we hired a car and went out to the desert. We went to Valley of Fire, where the colours were extraordinary. We were driving back towards dusk and all the rocks were turning different colours, and I held this within me. When I got back to New York, there was a giant canvas conveniently waiting, and I painted that painting the very next day. And this is something I do a lot. I see something, and have a feeling of something – it might be the light, or the heat, they are very specific in that sense – and I unload the painting. Anyway this one came out like this, first time, because it was ready.'

Being ready is important to making great art, but Scully isn't someone who waits idly for the afflatus to take his hand.

Wall of Light Desert Night, 1999

Planes of Light, 1999

12.01.04

Painting

Its hard to keep it going. Since
it feeds on such deep emotional
and physical resources: and its
normal to get tired, and to
admit to getting tired! And its
hard resist that. The seduction
of fatigue. And to let go of
some of what it is, But like a
lot of other things in the world: it
is what it is; exactly. And its
not, what its not. With painting: there's'
paint, and there's brushes and there's.
canvas. And thats' what it is. Its
easy to say, and not so easy to do.

Handwritten page, 'Painting', 2004

Inspiration and breakthroughs – like the moment on the beach in Mexico, or the eureka effect in his studio near the Old Kent Road in 1997 – come to him because he makes himself available almost incessantly. Though he is very good at reflecting on art, he is even better at making it.

ss   It's a lot easier to talk about drawing than it is to draw. I had a friend in England – this goes back a long way – and he was an absolute left-wing, borderline anarchist, who lived in a place that was a complete bohemian mess; the kind of person I used to hang out with when I was young. I used to hang out with the hippie brigade because we were protesting all the time against apartheid and the Vietnam War and all that stuff. We were extremely political. And this friend of mine used to use his sofa's arms as ashtrays. So instead of having an ashtray, he burned ashtrays into the arms of the sofa. Then he would empty the astray by just scooping up all the fag ends with his hands and throwing them away.

kg   Sounds cosy.

ss   It was cosy. This guy – his name was Niall Martin – wanted to go to art school. He begged me to get him into art school. He was a great talker. I was teaching at Goldsmiths [London], which later on, of course, became a coven for conceptual art, where they would throw painters into a cooking pot and cook them and eat them and make conceptual art out of what was left of their belongings. Terrible place! But anyway, when I taught there, I taught with Basil Beattie, who is an old friend of mine and a wonderful painter. I have a big painting by Basil in my collection, I'm happy to say. So I get Niall Martin into Goldsmiths, right, and there he is, sitting down, and he's got a canvas in front of him that's not too big and not too small. Just right, as Goldilocks would say. It was about 40 × 40 inches, a perfectly manageable size. He was

Between Two Lights, 1999

Four Large Mirrors, 1999

sitting there in the class that I was teaching – a foundation class – and he started talking about what a painting was, and what a painting meant, and how to start a painting. The right way to start a painting, he said, had to be thought about very seriously because, once you started painting, everything that was added to the painting subsequently would be affected by its beginning, which seemed to me to be a pretty tight philosophical argument. Niall was certainly a talker, and he was a thinker. The next week I came in, and he was sitting in front of that blank canvas, talking about the reality of painting and how a painting was a manifestation of an action and the physical result of something that was a signifier of a position in the culture. Indeed, all these words rang true. I couldn't disagree with any of it. But, at a certain point, painting requires non-analytical, faith-based action driven by will, because every painting reaches a crisis point where you have to push it on through. Anyway, this kind of philosophical confrontation between Niall and the blank canvas went on for weeks until he got up one day and left art school and didn't come back. He was the perfect proof that it's a lot easier to talk about drawing than it is to draw.

KG   Well, had Niall stayed a little longer, been there when conceptualism really got going at Goldsmiths, his talked-about-but-never-executed blank canvas would have been a masterpiece.

SS   He would have been the star of the school. He would have been its philosopher – its nihilistic philosopher. He would have been able to justify that not doing something was, in and of itself, the most profound action possible. There it is: a salutary lesson for all gasbags. At a certain point, it requires an irrational attachment to action to get something done. I always loved that film by Werner Herzog, *Fitzcarraldo*, where they pushed the steamship over the mountain because they wanted to hear opera in the jungle. That requires getting that damn steamship over that bloody mountain. What they're saying in the film is that it takes sweat and belief and will and madness in order to create a moment of sublime beauty.

KG Art is doing something you should know better than to do.

SS Yeah, I did the same thing myself in a way with *Any Questions*. That damn painting always had questions.

Scully is referring to a pivotal work from 1984, a large (and very heavy) black, grey and bone-white painting in oil on linen. With its protruding left-hand panel of wide vertical stripes, the work feels very much connected to other paintings made around this time, including *Paul* (1984) and *The Bather* (1983). But the opposite side of the work, composed of six smaller sections – each with four grey and white stripes – tethered together haphazardly, this way and that, leaving a ragged edge on the right of the painting, anticipates the 'Wall of Light' configurations that were still to come. 'I called it *Any Questions*', Scully said in a lecture he delivered at Oxford University in 1985, 'because I went to see a concert with Talking Heads, a beautiful concert. At the end David Byrne said, "Any questions?" As if you were going to have any questions about punk rock 'n' roll! What I did with this painting was two different things. I put the panels together in a way that one couldn't really answer questions about. I thought of the right side as the same as the left side, only broken up and put back together again. So when I think about these paintings, I don't think about them in terms of patterns. I know that they are patterns because they are repeated structures, but really I am thinking about different kinds of thought structures... One kind of repetition juxtaposed with another kind of repetition – that is how you spend your day in the city – the endless repetition of life, or expression, or beauty, or mystery, without avoiding what it fundamentally is.'

Any Questions, 1984–2005

The Bather, 1983

ss At one point I lifted up the painting and gave myself a hernia. I made the mistake of hiring an Irishman in Germany, a very nice guy called Jerry Darcy. But Jerry refused to lift the heavy end of the painting, even though he was twenty years my junior...

KG ...and hired to lift the painting...

ss ...and paid to lift the painting by me! There we were in the middle of the Bavarian countryside in my wonderful studio, with an Irishman who's telling me that he can't lift the heavy end of the painting. Since there were only two of us, and there were two ends to the painting, one of us had to be on the heavy end. It turned out that it was me. It turned out also that Jerry has a much stronger sense of caution than I do. However, Jerry is not a famous artist and there is the connection with Niall, which is, by the way, another Irish name. Niall who couldn't act. I, of course, act too much. I have an excess of action. So I get on the heavy end of the painting, and when I lifted it I remember thinking that it required literally all of me. It took my body and soul to move that painting. Two weeks later I woke up with a plum in my belly button, which required me to have an operation.

Every atom in my body was engaged. Not one part of me could tap out. So Jerry was very wise. But making art is not about being wise. It's about belief and love and passion, as are most things extraordinary such as going to Antarctica or finding the source of the Nile or writing a wonderful play. All these things require a kind of mad effort. Being sensible and making something magnificent, creatively, do not go together, do they?

KG Do you agree with William Faulkner when he said that the writer's, or artist's, 'only responsibility is to his art'? Faulkner says the writer 'will be completely ruthless if he is a good one... Everything goes by the board: honor, pride, decency, security, happiness, all, to get the book written. If a writer has to rob his mother, he will not hesitate; the "Ode on a Grecian Urn" is worth any number of old ladies.'

ss Wow! I don't agree with that, though, because the embrace of my beautiful son has caused my level of creativity to rise exponentially. And here's a story about an old lady – a very beautiful story that, I think, affected me greatly, and not in a sad way at all. It taught me something about grace. Grace, humanity, consideration and kindness were all manifested by this old lady, and you just reminded me of it. So when somebody says the 'Ode on a Grecian Urn' is worth any number of old ladies, I don't agree.

I was outside 82 Highbury Hill with my two cousins and my little brother. We used to sit in a tree that had these elderflower berries on it. The berries are dark, dark, dark red – a beautiful red that you often find in my paintings now, by the way. This nearly black red, I think, comes from the tree that used to be outside the house. We never used it to make elderflower anything. I don't know why, but now I certainly would if I had this tree. Anyway, these flying ants used to get on it, and they would walk up our legs and inside our short trousers. They drove us crazy, but we would never give up getting in the tree. We loved that tree.

One day, we were all sitting in it, and an old lady came along and stopped right opposite. To this day, there are low walls outside those houses that are capped by Yorkshire stone, and you can sit on them. They're kind of bench height. So I saw this old lady come along and sit down. We were kind children, you know. We were always taught to be very kind, particularly by my extremely religious grandmother, Ellen.

Scully adored his grandmother and holds in his mind a very clear and poignant portrait of her. In 2016, when I was helping him to

my grandmother ELLEN looked like Geronimo,
the great apache warrior, who resisted
the oppression of the U.S army. She seemed,
to me, to be made out of the same
moral material & Her nose was roman.
straight, like my fathers, and forever
pointing forward. Contructed for direction
and certainly, Her eyes, stayed behind,
in their deep sad sockets, They had,
it seemed to me, caught all the
world's sorrows, And they were holding
them, for the sake of others, She
sang in pubs, and people bought her
drinks, so she would sing more. For
she was noble, and capable of a
goodness, that others wanted to look
at. Since it was a thing of moving
beauty.

Handwritten page, 'Ellen', 2016

compile a volume of his selected writings, he was moved to compose a fresh tribute to her. It is an affecting piece, and one that he has since struggled to read aloud without being overcome when we organize readings from the volume, as we have in London and Dublin. 'My grandmother looked like Geronimo, the great Apache warrior who resisted the oppression of the US Army,' the piece memorably begins. 'She seemed, to me, to be made out of the same moral material. Her nose was Roman, straight, like my father's, and forever pointing forward. Constructed for direction and certainty. Her eyes stayed behind, in their deep, sad sockets. They had, it seemed to me, caught all the world's sorrows. And they were holding them for the sake of others. She sang in pubs, and people bought her drinks so she would sing more. For she was noble, and capable of a goodness that others wanted to look at. Since it was a thing of moving beauty.'

ss I ran over to see this old lady, to ask if she was all right. She said she was all right, but then she said, 'Do you think you could get me a glass of water, darling?' 'Yeah, of course I'll get you a glass of water,' I said, and I ran over to the house and brought her one. She had a little drink, and she was so sweet, kind, polite and considerate to me. She said things like 'Oh, thank you, darling', 'Be careful when you cross the road', 'Oh, that's great' and 'That's so kind of you. You're such a good boy'. She was almost angelic. And the reason is because the angels were coming to take her away. She simply, quietly died right in front of me. It taught me something incredible about grace, and it affected me incredibly. To this day, it nearly breaks my heart to recount the story. She was so lovely. So here's another thing that I don't agree with, and that's when Picasso said that art is war. Art is not war. War is war. Art is the enemy of war. Art is love.

Scully family, 2014

Land Sea Sky, 1999

Sean Scully's Life and Work

1945 Born in Dublin, Ireland, on 30 June. In order to have an address for the birth certificate, Scully's family is taken off the street into a 7×7 ft room at 7 Thomas Davis Street West, in Inchicore, a working-class neighbourhood west of Dublin's city centre.

1945–49 Among travellers, Scully's family shuttles back and forth between Dublin and London.

1949 Family settles permanently in London, initially in the Old Kent Road, south of the capital. Scully's father, John, is absent for eight months, serving time for desertion.

1950 Family lodges in a room at Scully's grandmother's house in Highbury, north London.

1953 Family moves to Sydenham, south London. The future artist opens a clinic for injured animals in the family house.

1954 Scully is greatly affected by the paintings he sees in Catholic churches and decides to become an artist at the age of nine.

1958–59 Becomes interested in American Rhythm & Blues music and starts a music club of his own. Involved with gangs and petty criminality. Briefly joins notorious street gang the 'Sydenham Six'.

1960–64 Apprentices at a printmaking factory in Notting Hill, London, working as a typesetter. Quits apprenticeship and joins Finnemore & Field, a graphic design studio near Chancery Lane.

– Attends evening classes at the Central School of Art, London, with an interest in figurative painting.

– Regularly visits Vincent van Gogh's painting *Van Gogh's Chair* (1888) at Tate Gallery, London.

1965 On 7 May 1965 Scully becomes a father at the age of 19, with the birth of his son Paul.

1965–68 Decides to dedicate himself entirely to art studies. Studies at Croydon School of Art, London. Discovers abstract expressionism.

1968–72 Attends Newcastle University, Newcastle-upon-Tyne, England.

1969 A Newcastle University Theatre production of Samuel Beckett's *Waiting for Godot* makes a lasting impression on him.

– Visits Morocco. The stripes and colours of local textiles and carpets and the southern light leave a lasting an impression. Begins to experiment with sculpture.

– His paintings consist of complicated grid systems of intersecting bands and lines that reveal the influence of Op Art.

1970 Awarded the Peter Stuyvesant Foundation Prize.

1971 Marries Rosemary Purnell. Remains at Newcastle University as a teaching assistant. Spends one day a week teaching art at the City of Sunderland College of Art, Houghton-le-Spring, England.

1972–73 Makes his first visit to the United States as a recipient of the prestigious Frank Knox Fellowship at Harvard University, Cambridge, MA. Begins using tape and spraying paint in constructing grids of interlaced vertical, horizontal and diagonal bands and stripes.

1973 Holds first solo exhibition at the Rowan Gallery, London, selling out the entire show.

1973–75 Teaches at the Chelsea College of Art and Design and Goldsmiths, London.

1975 Moves to New York after being awarded a two-year Harkness Fellowship. Continues to explore the potential of minimalism.

1977 Secures first solo exhibition in New York at the Duffy-Gibbs Gallery.

1978 Marries Catherine Lee.

1978–82 Teaches part-time at Princeton University, New Jersey, USA. Colour palette is reduced to shades of grey monochrome and composition is pared down to thin horizontal or vertical lines.

1980 Travels to Mexico. Inspired by the trip, begins painting from nature.

1981 Offered his first retrospective at the Ikon Gallery, Birmingham, England. Begins to reject minimalist aesthetics by reinstating into his paintings colour, space, metaphor and expression. Stops taping his stripes and begins drawing them freehand. Brushstrokes are clearly visible. Achieves breakthrough with the multipanel painting *Backs and Fronts*.

– Teaches at the Parsons School of Design (1981–84), New York, USA.

1982 Reaches maturity with *Heart of Darkness*. Combines rigid geometry with expressive texture and colour.

– Continues to combine and recombine canvases to make polyptychs.

1983 Becomes an American citizen

– Paul, his 18-year-old son, dies in a car accident in London.

– Receives the Guggenheim Fellowship.

1984 Dedicates his painting *Paul* to his deceased son.

– Creates the first 'Wall of Light', a watercolour that will eventually inspire an extended, and still ongoing, meditation on architecture and light from the late 1990s.

– Receives the National Endowment for the Arts Fellowship.
– Selected for the exhibition 'An International Survey of Recent Painting and Sculpture' at the Museum of Modern Art, New York.

1985 First solo American museum exhibition at the Carnegie Museum of Art, Pittsburgh, PA, which then travels to the Museum of Fine Arts, Boston, MA.

1987 Switches to a less complex, flatter and smaller scale of working.
– Makes several visits to Mexico (1987–90). Time spent at Maya historical sites provides inspiration for later stone sculptures.

1989 First solo exhibition in a European museum, Whitechapel Gallery, London; travels to Palacio de Velázquez, Madrid, and Städtische Galerie im Lenbachhaus, Munich.

1990 Maurice Poirier's monograph is published by Hudson Hills Press, New York.

1991 Begins regular use of the chequerboard motif.

1992 Lectures at Harvard.
– In December, revisits Morocco to make a film for the BBC on Matisse, who visited Morocco in 1912–13.

1994 Establishes new studio in Barcelona, Spain.

1995 Participates in the Joseph Beuys Lectures on the state of contemporary art in Britain, Europe and the United States.

1996 Visits Morocco.

1997 Creates large oil painting *Because of the Other*, a bridge between the small watercolour *Wall of Light* made in Mexico and the acclaimed series of large-scale canvases collectively entitled 'Wall of Light'.

2000 Becomes an Honorary Fellow of the London Institute of Arts and Letters.

2001 Becomes a member of Aosdána, an Irish affiliation of artists engaged in literature, music and the visual arts.

2002 Becomes Professor of painting at the Akademie der Bildenden Künste (2002–7), Munich, Germany.

2003 Receives Honorary doctorates from the Massachusetts College of Art and Design, Boston, and the National University of Ireland, Dublin.
– Commissioned to make a site-specific sculpture for the University of Limerick, titled *Crann Saoilse*.
– Retrospective exhibition opens at Sara Hildén Art Museum Tampere, Finland; travels to Neues Museum Weimar, Weimar, and National Gallery of Australia, Canberra.

2005 'Sean Scully: Wall of Light' exhibition opens at The Phillips Collection, Washington, DC, and travels to the Modern Art Museum of Fort Worth, Fort Worth, TX, Cincinnati Art Museum, Cincinnati, OH, and the Metropolitan Museum of Art, New York.
– Artist travels to the Aran Islands, off the west coast of Ireland, with students from the Munich Kunstakademie and makes a series of photographs of the islands' stone walls.

2006 Marries artist Liliane Tomasko.
– Dublin City Gallery – The Hugh Lane, Dublin, opens the Sean Scully Gallery, a permanent room devoted exclusively to work by the artist.
– Exhibition of prints at the Bibliothèque Nationale de France, Paris.

2007-8 'Sean Scully: A Retrospective' opens at Miró Foundation, Barcelona; travels to Musée d'Art Moderne, Saint-Étienne, and Museo d'Arte Contemporanea di Roma, Rome.
– Awarded position of Doctor Honoris Causa by the Universidad Miguel Hernández in Valencia, Spain.
– Gives Elson Lecture at the National Gallery of Art, Washington, DC.
– Commissioned to make *Wall of Light Cubed*, a site-specific stone sculpture for Château La Coste near Aix-en-Provence, France.

2009 Retrospective exhibition 'Konstantinopel oder die versteckte Sinnlichkeit. Die Bilderwelt von Sean Scully (Constantinople or the Sensual Concealed: The Imagery of Sean Scully)' opens at MKM Museum Küppersmühle für Moderne Kunst, Duisburg; travels to Ulster Museum, Belfast.
– Son Oisin is born.

2010-11 'Sean Scully: Works from the 1980s' opens at VISUAL – Centre for Contemporary Art, Carlow, Ireland; travels to Leeds Art Gallery, Leeds, and Wilhelm-Hack-Museum, Ludwigshafen am Rhein, Germany.
– Chazen Museum of Art, Madison, WI, opens their new expansion with solo exhibition of Scully's eight-part *Liliane* paintings and related works.

2012 Opens nine solo museum exhibitions from Philadelphia, PA, to Rome, Italy, including 'Sean Scully: Grey Wolf – A Retrospective' at the Kunstmuseum Bern, Switzerland, and Lentos Kunstmuseum, Linz, Austria.
– Becomes a member of the Royal Academy of Arts in London, England.

2014 Awarded an honorary Doctorate of Fine Art from the National University of Ireland's Burren College of Art.
– His painting *Green Robe Figure* (2005) is included in the exhibition 'Post-Picasso. Reacciones Contemporáneas' at the Picasso Museum, Barcelona. The exhibition examines

the responses of contemporary artists to the life and work of Pablo Picasso.

– Extends his 'Landline' series, started in 2000. A majority of the work is done on aluminium panels, composed of horizontal stripes using colours that reference his student period.

2015 Opens fourteen solo exhibitions around the world.

– Museum Liaunig in Neuhaus, Austria, opens their new building expansion with a solo exhibition 'Sean Scully: Painting as an Imaginative World Appropriation'.

– Participates for the first time at the Venice Biennale with the solo exhibition 'Sean Scully: Land Sea' at Palazzo Falier in Venice.

– Opens a new studio space in Tappan, New York.

– Publishes a new book of essays by Arthur C. Danto on Sean Scully.

– His permanent installation at the 10th-century Church of Santa Cecília de Montserrat in Barcelona, Spain, opens to the public. Receives the award V Congreso Protecturi, Madrid, Spain, for his contribution to Spanish religious heritage.

– A new sculpture in Corten steel, *Boxes of Air*, is made for a solo exhibition focusing on sculpture at Château La Coste, France. Five more sculptures are produced, further developing this expression in depth.

2016 Revisits the techniques first introduced in the late 1960s with spray painting.

– Receives *Harper's Bazaar* Art International Artist of the Year Award.

– Work expands in two particular directions: sculpture and figuration.

– *Inner: The Collected Writings and Selected Interviews of Sean Scully*, edited by Kelly Grovier, is published by Hatje Cantz.

2017 First solo exhibition in Russia is held at MAMM, the Multimedia Art Museum, Moscow, and then travels to the State Russian Museum, the Marble Palace, St Petersburg.

2018 Made an Honorary Doctor of Letters by Newcastle University, Newcastle, England.

– Solo exhibition of sculpture at the Cuadra San Cristóbal, Mexico City, is the first and only exhibition ever staged at the Luis Barragán masterpiece, and includes paintings installed in the working stable block.

– A 40-metre-long mosaic installation is unveiled at the new American Embassy in London.

– The first exhibition dedicated to sculpture, 'Inside Outside', opens at the Yorkshire Sculpture Park in Wakefield, England. Six new sculptures were made for the exhibition, including the monumental *Wall Dale Cubed*,

consisting of over 1,000 tonnes of local Yorkshire stone. *Crate of Air*, a continuation of the 'Boxes of Air' series, was rethought and reconceived into smaller modular parts, enabling the artist to reform and reconstruct the sculpture depending on its location.

– Two further major exhibitions of painting open. 'Vita Duplex', a retrospective, opens at the Staatliche Kunsthalle Karlsruhe. The Hirshhorn Museum and Sculpture Garden in Washington, DC, opens a solo exhibition of the 'Landline' series.

2019 The National Gallery in London, UK, opens a solo exhibition of new work titled 'Sea Star', responding to the museum's collection of Turner paintings.

– *Unstoppable: Sean Scully and the Art of Everything*, a BBC documentary on the life and work of the artist, is released, directed by award-winning documentary filmmaker Nick Willing.

– San Giorgio Maggiore in Venice invites Scully to make a site-specific intervention in the Holy space and accompanying exhibition in their associated buildings, in conjunction with the 58th Biennale di Venezia. The exhibition is of landmark importance in the artist's career, with a sculpture 10 metres high in the central nave of the 16th-century church, accompanied by an illuminated manuscript containing over forty unique drawings.

– A solo exhibition 'Long Light' opens at the Villa Panza in Varese, Italy, and the exhibition 'Vita Duplex' travels to the LWL-Museum, Münster, Germany.

– The Albertina Museum in Vienna dedicates a solo exhibition to 'Eleuthera', the series that begins the artist's return to figuration.

2020 Painted during the first month of the coronavirus pandemic, *Black Windows* and *Black Square* become immediately recognized as significant to the moment.

– New sculptures using glass and mirror-polished aluminium form the exhibition 'Inside Outside' at fellow artist and friend Tony Cragg's Skulpturenpark Waldfrieden.

– The Hungarian National Gallery, Budapest, opens a major retrospective of Sean Scully, which will travel to the Benaki Museum, Athens.

2021 A major fifty-year career retrospective 'Sean Scully: The Shape of Ideas', organized by the Philadelphia Museum of Art, to open at the Modern Art Museum of Fort Worth, Texas, and then in Philadelphia in 2022.

– Currently lives and works between New York and Germany.

Notes

p. **11** 'There's something wrong with this picture': Sean Scully, *Inner: The Collected Writings and Selected Interviews of Sean Scully*, edited by Kelly Grovier (Ostfildern: Hatja Cantz, 2016), p. 88

p. **13** 'the 22-year-old who authored them': cf. Kelly Grovier's discussion of Scully's abstract figuration in the exhibition catalogue *Sean Scully: Facing East*, Palace Editions, St Petersburg, 2017

p. **24** 'a battered stretch of blood-stained linen': Kelly Grovier, 'Thirteen Ways of Looking at a Landline', *Sean Scully: Land Sea*, Skira, Milan, 2015, p. 100

p. **27** 'an image of transcendental repose': *Inner*, op. cit., pp. 282–84

p. **28** 'but it's all in the service of stealing': *Inner*, op. cit., p. 160

p. **35** 'I had a tenacious intellect': *Inner*, op. cit., p. 286

p. **43** 'Scully set about saving painting': see Kelly Grovier's discussion of Scully's contribution to contemporary art in *Sean Scully: The Shape of Ideas*, Philadelphia Museum of Art, 2020

p. **46** 'Scully's return to figuration': see Kelly Grovier's discussion of Scully's two figurative series 'Eleuthera' and 'Madonna' in the exhibition catalogue *Sean Scully: Human*, Skira Editore, Milan, 2020

p. **49** 'an art work should be profound and timeless': *Inner*, op. cit., p. 35

p. **57** 'the fourth most proficient barber in Britain': *Inner*, op. cit., p. 288

p. **59** 'the alter ego of a troubled soul': Rachel Spence, 'Sean Scully: "England is a country that basically doesn't understand art"', *Financial Times*, 21 September 2018

p. **64** 'that I learned through her': *Inner*, op. cit., pp. 92–93

p. **64** 'As beautiful as you': Don McLean, 'Vincent', *American Pie*, 1971

p. **67** 'a king equipped with urbane wit and cool style': *Inner*, op. cit., pp. 297–98

p. **71** 'the flow of lonesome rivers': Righteous Brothers, 'Unchained Melody', music by Alex North and lyrics by Hy Zaret, 1965

p. **71** 'it also floats back, in return': *Inner*, op. cit., p. 294

p. **81** 'I needed that space': *Inner*, op. cit., p. 127

p. **92** 'open it up mentally': *Inner*, op. cit., p. 31

p. **95** 'a revolutionary from the inside': *Inner*, op. cit., pp. 270–71

p. **97** 'A wall of light': *Inner*, op. cit., p. 109

p. **109** 'as interesting as the rightness': *Inner*, op. cit., p. 211

p. **141** 'Starry, starry night': Don McLean, 'Vincent', *American Pie*, 1971

p. **149** 'the world continues on its merry slide': *Inner*, op. cit., p. 117

p. **153** 'I come from a musical family': *Inner*, op. cit., p. 288

p. **161** T. S. Eliot, 'The Hollow Men', *Poems, 1909–1925*, London: Faber & Gwyer, 1925

p. **173** 'the finality of final breaths': Kelly Grovier, *Sean Scully at the National Gallery of Ireland*, catalogue for the exhibition 9 May–20 September 2015, National Gallery of Ireland, Dublin, pp. 27–28

p. **183** 'he came around to it': *Inner*, op. cit., pp. 272–73

p. **189** 'the frenetic flinging of Jackson Pollock': Kelly Grovier, 'A painter earns his stripes', *Times Literary Supplement*, 15 January 2010, p. 17

p. **196** 'down into the ditch he's in': Bob Dylan, 'It's Alright Ma (I'm Only Bleeding)', *Bringing It All Back Home*, 1965

p. **196** 'Scully's reminiscences and views': Bob Dylan, 'I Contain Multitudes', *Rough and Rowdy Ways*, 2020

p. **216** 'something you can recognize': *Inner*, op. cit., p. 176

p. **225** 'to pink in the morning': *Inner*, op. cit., p. 187

p. **236** 'without avoiding what it fundamentally is': *Inner*, op. cit., pp. 44–45

p. **240** 'any number of old ladies': Jean Stein, interview with William Faulkner, *Paris Review*, Issue 12, Spring, 1956

p. **242** 'a thing of moving beauty': *Inner*, op. cit., p. 324

List of Illustrations

a = above, b = below

1 *Adoration* (detail), 1982. Oil on canvas, linen and wood, 274.3×396.2 cm (108×156 in.); 2 *Windows* (detail), 1980–81. Oil on canvas, 106.7×106.7 cm (42×42 in.); 7 Kelly Grovier and Sean Scully. Photograph by Andrey Gertsev; 10 *Untitled*, 1966. Oil pastel on paper, 40.4×30.5 cm (16×12 in.). Private collection. Image courtesy of Lisson Gallery, New York; 12 The Scully family, with Sean's cousins Lesley and Anna, 1949; 14 *Figure in a Room*, 1967. Oil on canvas, 170.8×164.5 cm (67¼ ×64¾ in.). Private collection; 15 *Untitled (Seated Figure)*, 1967. Oil on canvas, 105.4×74.9 cm (41½×29½ in.). Private collection. Photograph by Rob Carter; 16 *Three Women Bearing Arms I*, 1966–67. Oil pastel on paper, 27.6×37.5 cm (10⅞×14⅞ in.). Private collection; 17 'What Art Is', 2004. Ink on paper, 29.7×21 cm (11¾×8⅜ in.). Private collection. Photograph by Sean Scully Studio; 18 *Abstract Two Blues*, 1965–66. Gouache on paper, 45×61 cm (17¾×24 in.). Private collection. Photograph by Christoph Knoch; 20 *Landline Skyline*, 2014. Oil on aluminium, 215.9×190.5 cm (85×75 in.). Private collection. Photograph by Robert Bean; 21 *Landline Blue Veined*, 2016. Oil on linen, 208.3×193 cm (82×76 in.). Private collection. Photograph by Robert Bean; 22 Vincent van Gogh, *Van Gogh's Chair*, 1888. Oil on canvas, 91.8×73 cm (36¼×28¾ in.). The National Gallery, London. Bought, Courtauld Fund, 1924. Photo The National Gallery, London/Scala, Florence; 26 *Child with Dove for Oisin*, 2013. Oil and pencil on linen, 81.3×71.1 cm (32×28 in.). Private collection. Photograph by Frank Hutter; 31a *Blanket Hung Above Chair*, 1964. Mixed media on paper, 47.6×31.1 cm (18¾×12¼ in.). Private collection. Photograph by Christoph Knoch; 31b *Two Figures, Interior Scene*, 1964. Pencil, coloured pencil and pastel on paper, 38.1×55.9 cm (15×22 in.). Private collection. Photograph by Frank Hutter; 32 *Cactus*, 1964. Oil on canvas, 33×27.9 cm (13×11 in.). Private collection. Photograph by John Webb; 34 *Gray Zig Zag*, 1970. Acrylic on canvas, 243.8×274.3 cm (96×108 in.). Private collection. Photograph by John Webb; 36 *Bend 1*, 1968. Oil pastel on paper, 27.9×48.9 cm (11×19¼ in.). Private collection; 37 *Square*, 1969. Acrylic on canvas, 205.7×205.7 cm (81×81 in.). Private collection; 39 *Bridge*, 1970. Acrylic on canvas, 274.3×182.9 cm (108×72 in.).

Private collection; 40–41 *Backs and Fronts*, 1981. Oil on linen and canvas, 243.8×609.6 cm (96×240 in.). Private collection. Image courtesy Magonza. Photograph by Michele Alberto Sereni; 42 *Blue*, 1981. Oil on canvas, 207×213.4 cm (81½×84 in.). Sean Scully, *Blue*, 1981, Oil on canvas, 213.4×207 cm, Collection Irish Museum of Modern Art, Purchase, 2006; 45 *Madonna*, 2019. Oil and oil pastel on aluminium, 215.9×190.5 cm (85×75 in.). Private collection. Photograph by Robert Bean; 48 Piet Mondrian, *Composition*, 1921. Oil on canvas, 49.5×49.5 cm (19½×19½ in.). The Metropolitan Museum of Art, New York. Jacques and Natasha Gelman Collection, 1998. Photo Malcolm Varon/The Metropolitan Museum of Art/Art Resource/Scala, Florence; 53 *A Bedroom in Venice*, 1988. Oil on linen, 243.8×304.8 cm (96×120 in.). The Museum of Modern Art (MoMA), New York, USA. Fractional and promised gift of Agnes Gund; 54 *No Neo*, 1984. Oil on linen, 243.8×304.8 cm (96×120 in.). Private collection; 60 *Black Square*, 2020. Oil on aluminium, 215.9×190.5 cm (85×75 in.). Private collection. Photograph by Elisabeth Bernstein; 62 *Untitled (Newcastle #1)*, 1969. Acrylic on canvas, dimensions unknown. No longer extant; 65 *Vincent*, 2002. Oil on linen, 190.5×203.2 cm (75×80 in.). Private collection. Photograph by Zindman/Fremont; 68 *Blaze*, 1971. Acrylic on canvas, 215.9×388 cm (85×152¾ in.). Private collection; 69 *Newcastle Boogie-Woogie*, 1971. Acrylic on canvas, 182.9×365.8 cm (72×144 in.). No longer extant; 73 *Fourth Layer – Tooley Street*, 1973. Acrylic on canvas, 244×244 cm (96⅛×96⅛ in.). Ulster Museum, National Museums of Northern Ireland, Belfast, Northern Ireland, UK. Courtesy National Museums Northern Ireland; 74a *Crossover Painting #1*, 1974. Acrylic on canvas, 243.5×243.5 cm (96×96 in.). Private collection; 74b *Taped Painting Cream and Black*, 1975. Acrylic and tape on canvas, 243.8×243.8 cm (96×96 in.). Private collection. Photograph by John Webb; 77 Paul Huxley, *Untitled no. 128*, 1971. Acrylic on canvas, 195.5×195.5 cm (77×77 in.). The Whitworth, Manchester. Photo courtesy The Whitworth, The University of Manchester. © Paul Huxley; 78 *East Coast Light 2*, 1973. Acrylic on canvas, 215.3×243.8 cm (84¾×96 in.). Private collection; 80 *Harvard Frame Painting*, 1972. Acrylic, sacking, resin, felt and wood, 182.9×182.9 cm (72×72 in.). Private collection. Photograph by Elisabeth

249

Bernstein; **85** Sean Scully in his Duane Street studio, New York, 1980; **86a** *Heart of Darkness*, 1982. Oil on linen, 243.8×365.8 cm (96×144 in.). Art Institute of Chicago, Chicago, Illinois, USA. Gift of Society for Contemporary Art; **86b** *Adoration*, 1982. Oil on canvas, linen and wood, 274.3×396.2 cm (108×156 in.). Private collection. Photograph by Alan Zindman; **87** *Blame*, 1983. Oil on linen, 268×267.3 cm (105 ½×105 ¼ in.). Whitney Museum of American Art, New York, USA. Promised gift of Jon Sobel and Marcia Dunn. Photograph by Michael Bodycomb; **89** *Angel*, 1983. Oil on linen, 243.8×274.3 cm (96×108 in.). Iris & B. Gerald Cantor Center for Visual Arts at Stanford University, Stanford, California, USA. Given in gratitude for Tom Seligman's leadership, vision and friendship, by Jill and John Freidenrich and the Robert and Ruth Halperin Foundation; **90** *Come In*, 1983. Oil on linen, 246.4×304.8 cm (97×120 in.). Private collection; **91** *Heat*, 1984. Oil on linen, 274.3×243.8 cm (108×96 in.). The Gertsev Collection, Moscow, Russia; **94** Cimabue, *Madonna Enthroned with the Child, Saint Francis and Four Angels*, *c.* 1278–80. Fresco, 320×340 cm (126×133 ⅞ in.). Basilica of Saint Francis of Assisi; **96** Detail from *Aran*, 2005. Suite of 24 photographs, 40.6×50.8 cm (16×20 in.) each; **98a** *Arran*, 1986. Oil on linen, 101.6×121.9 cm (40×48 in.). Private collection; **98b** *Arran*, 1990. Oil on wood, 30.6×29.2 cm (12×11 ½ in.). Private collection; **99** *Wall of Light Arran*, 2002. Oil on linen, 182.9×213.4 cm (72×84 in.). Museo Nacional Centro de Arte Reina Sofía, Madrid, Spain; **101** 'The Dire Fire', date unknown. Ink on paper, dimensions unknown. Private collection; Photograph by Sean Scully Studio; **103** Sean Scully, the hills of Wicklow, June 1983; **104** *Inisheer*, 1990–96. Oil on linen, 91.5×91.5 cm (36×36 in.). Private collection. Photograph by Lee Welch; **107** 'I Agree with Nietsche', 2007. Ink on paper, 29.5×21 cm (11 ⅝×8 ¼ in.); Private collection. Photograph by Sean Scully Studio; **108** *Falling Wrong*, 1985. Oil on linen, 243.8×274.3 cm (96×108 in.). Private collection; **112** Jasper Johns, *0 through 9*, 1961. Oil on linen, 137.2×105.1 cm (54×41 ⅜ in.); Whitney Museum of American Art, New York. Gift of The American Contemporary Art Foundation, Inc., Leonard A. Lauder, President. Photo Whitney Museum of American Art/Licensed by Scala. © Jasper Johns/VAGA at ARS, NY and DACS, London 2021; **113** Jean-Baptiste-Siméon Chardin, *A Bowl of Plums*, *c.* 1728. Oil on canvas, 44.5×56.2 cm (17 ½×22 ⅛ in.). The Phillips Collection, Washington, DC. Acquired 1920; **115–16** 'The Sculpture', 2009. Ink on paper, 29.5×21 cm (11 ⅝×8 ¼ in.) each. Private collection. Photograph by Sean Scully Studio; **120** *For Charles Choset*, 1988. Oil on linen, 190.5×228.6 cm (75×90 in.). Private collection; **121** Charles Choset at Scully's Duane Street studio, New York, 1981; **122** *1982 #4*, 1982. Watercolour on paper, 58.9×77.5 cm (23 ¼×30 ½ in.). Private collection. Photograph by Michael Bodycomb; **124** 'Backs and Fronts', 2016. Ink on paper, 29.5×21 cm (11 ⅝×8 ¼ in.). Private collection. Photograph by Sean Scully Studio; **125** Pablo Picasso, *Three Musicians*, 1921. Oil on canvas, 200.7×222.9 cm (79 ⅛×87 ⅞ in.). Museum of Modern Art, New York. Mrs Simon Guggenheim Fund. © Succession Picasso/DACS, London 2021; **127** *Precious*, 1981. Oil on canvas, 213.4×161 cm (84×63 ½ in.). Private collection. Photograph by Elisabeth Bernstein; **128** *Araby*, 1981. Oil on canvas, 243.8×198.1 cm (96×78 in.). Private collection; **129** *Fort #5*, 1980–81. Oil on canvas, 106.7×106.7 cm (42×42 in.). Private collection; **130** *Come and Go*, 1981. Oil on canvas, 213.4×236.2 cm (84×93 in.). Private collection. Photograph by Elisabeth Bernstein; **131** *Firebird*, 1980. Oil on canvas, 243.8×121.9 cm (96×48 in.). No longer extant; **133** *Enough*, 1981. Oil on canvas, 170×165 cm (67×65 in.). Private collection; **134** *Bonin*, 1982. Oil on Masonite with wood support, 45.7×62.2 cm (18×24 ½ in.). Private collection; **135** *A Day*, 1982. Oil on linen, 152.4×121.9 cm (60×48 in.). Private collection; **136** *Windows*, 1980–81. Oil on canvas, 106.7×106.7 cm (42×42 in.). Private collection; **139** *Star*, 2020. Oil on linen, 160×160 cm (63×63 in.). Private collection. Photograph by Elisabeth Bernstein; **140** Vincent van Gogh, *The Starry Night*, 1889. Oil on canvas. 73.7 cm × 92.1 cm (29×36 ¼ in.). Museum of Modern Art, New York. Acquired through the Lillie P. Bliss Bequest (by exchange). Conservation was made possible by the Bank of America Art Conservation Project; **142–43** *Arles Abend Vincent*, 2013. Oil on linen, 150×140 cm (59 ⅛×55 ⅛ in.) each. Private collection. Photograph by Christoph Knoch; **147** *Morocco*, 1969. Acrylic on canvas, 182.9×365.8 cm (72×144 in.). No longer extant; **148** *The Moroccan*, 1982. Oil on canvas, 284.5×160 cm (112×63 in.). Kemper Museum of Contemporary Art, Kansas City, Missouri, USA. Gift of the R. C. Kemper Charitable Trust; **151** Sean drawing on the beach, Essaouira, Morocco, 1996. Photograph by Bernd Klüser; **152a** *Mexico Malloy*, 1983. Watercolour on paper, 22.9×30.5 cm (9×12 in.). The Metropolitan Museum of Art, New York,

USA. Gift of the artist, 1997; **152b** *Mexico Christmas Day*, 1983. Watercolour on paper, 30.5 × 22.9 cm (12 × 9 in.). Collection of the Modern Art Museum of Fort Worth, Fort Worth, Texas, USA, made possible by a grant from Anne and John Marion; **155** *3.25.85 #1*, 1985. Watercolour on paper, 35.6 × 25.4 cm (14 × 10 in.). Private collection; **156** *Wall of Light 4.84*, 1984. Watercolour on paper, 22.9 × 30.5 cm (9 × 12 in.). National Gallery of Art, Washington, DC, USA. Gift of Jane P. Watkins; **158** *Breath*, 1987–90. Oil on linen, 182.9 × 182.9 cm (72 × 72 in.). Private collection; **162** *Durango*, 1990. Oil on linen, 289.5 × 457.2 × 15.9 cm (114 × 180 × 6 ⅜ in.). Kunstsammlung Nordrhein-Westfalen, Düsseldorf, Germany. Photograph by Trevor Good; **163** *Hammering*, 1990. Oil on linen, 279.4 × 441.9 cm (110 × 174 in.). Kunsthalle Bielefeld, Bielefeld, Germany; **164** 'Triptych', 2008. Ink on paper, 27.9 × 21.6 cm (11 × 8 ½ in.). Private collection. Photograph by Sean Scully Studio; **166** *Day Night*, 1990. Oil on linen, 254 × 381 cm (100 × 150 in.). Private collection; **167** *Winter Days*, 1990. Oil on linen, 305 × 229 × 14.4 cm (120 ⅛ × 90 ¼ × 5 ¾ in.). Private collection. Image courtesy of Kewenig Galerie, Berlin; **169** *Four Days*, 1990. Oil on linen, 274.3 × 365.8 cm (108 × 144 in.). Private collection; **170** *7.5.90*, 1990. Watercolour on paper, 55.9 × 76.2 cm (22 × 30 in.). Private collection; **171** 'Idea', 2006. Ink on paper, 24.5 × 21 cm (9 ⅝ × 8 ¼ in.). Private collection. Photograph by Sean Scully Studio; **172** *Paul*, 1984. Oil on linen, 259.1 × 320 cm (102 × 126 in.). Tate, London, UK. Presented by the Patrons of New Art through the Friends of the Tate Gallery 1986; **176** *Playground*, 2015. Ink and crayon on paper, 27.9 × 21.6 cm (11 × 8 ½ in.). Private collection. Photograph by Robert Bean; **177a** *Ghost Gun*, 2016. Oil and oil pastel on aluminium, 190.5 × 215.9 cm (75 × 85 in.). Private collection. Photograph by Robert Bean; **177b** *Ghost Night*, 2018. Oil and oil pastel on aluminium, 190.5 × 215.9 cm (75 × 85 in.). Private collection. Photograph by Robert Bean; **181** Oisin Scully within a painting, 2011; **182** *Eleuthera*, 2017. Oil and oil pastel on aluminium, 215.9 × 190.5 cm (85 × 75 in.). Private collection. Photograph by Robert Bean; **184** *Between You and Me*, 1988. Oil on linen with wood, 243.8 × 304.8 cm (96 × 120 in.). Albright-Knox Art Gallery, Buffalo, New York, USA. George Cary, Charles Clifton, James S. Ely and George B. and Jenny R. Mathews Funds, 1989; **185** *Spirit*, 1992. Oil on linen and steel, 198.1 × 411.5 cm (78 × 162 in.). Museo Nacional Centro de Arte Reina Sofía, Madrid, Spain; **187** *Long Night*, 1985. Oil on canvas and

wood, 245.1 × 325.8 cm (96 ½ × 128 ¼ in.). Private collection; **188** *Round and Round*, 1985. Oil on linen and wood, 236.2 × 299.7 cm (93 × 118 in.). The Doris and Donald Fisher Collection at the San Francisco Museum of Modern Art, San Francisco, California, USA; **190** *Liliane*, 2010. Oil on aluminium, 213.4 × 160 cm (84 × 63 in.) each. Private collection. Photograph by Etienne Frossard; **191** *Oisin's Breath*, 2010. Oil on linen, 160 × 160 cm (63 × 63 in.). Private collection. Photograph by Rob Carter; **195** 'Language of Light', 2000. Ink on paper, dimensions unknown. Private collection. Photograph by Sean Scully Studio; **199** Jean-Antoine Watteau, *Pilgrimage to the Isle of Cythera*, 1717. Oil on canvas, 129 × 194 cm (50 ⅞ × 48 ⅞ in.). Musée du Louvre, Paris; **200** Rembrandt, *Man in a Turban*, 1632. Oil on canvas, 152.7 × 111.1 cm (60 ⅛ × 43 ¾ in.). The Metropolitan Museum of Art. Bequest of William K. Vanderbilt, 1920; **201** Paul Klee, *May Picture*, 1925. Oil on cardboard, 42.2 × 49.5 cm (16 ⅝ × 19 ½ in.). The Metropolitan Museum of Art, New York. The Berggruen Klee Collection, 1984. Photo The Metropolitan Museum of Art/Art Resource/Scala, Florence; **203** St Matthew, from the *Book of Durrow* (MS. 57, fol. 21v), c. 650–700. Library of Trinity College Dublin. The Board of Trinity College Dublin; **204** *Boris and Gleb*, 1980. Oil on canvas, 243.8 × 88.9 cm (96 × 35 in.). Private collection. Photograph by Brian Buckley; **206** *Paul's Robe*, 2004. Oil on linen, 228.6 × 182.9 cm (90 × 72 in.). Private collection; **207** *Alberto's Robe*, 2004. Oil on linen, 228 × 183 cm (89 ⅞ × 72 in.). Private collection; **208a** *Yellow Robe 8.1.06*, 2006. Watercolour and pencil on paper, 56 × 48 cm (22 × 19 in.). Private collection. Photograph by Christoph Knoch; **208b** *Robe 3.26.08*, 2008. Watercolour on paper, 56.5 × 76.3 cm (22 ¼ × 30 in.). Private collection. Photograph by Christoph Knoch; **209** *Robe 4.1.19*, 2019. Watercolour and pencil on paper, 56.5 × 33 cm (22 ¼ × 13 in.). Private collection. Photograph by Brian Buckley; **210** 'Titian's Robe Pink', 2009. Ink on paper, dimensions unknown. Private collection. Photograph by Sean Scully Studio; **211** *Titian's Robe Pink 08*, 2008. Oil on aluminium, 279.5 × 406.5 cm (110 × 160 in.). Private collection. Photograph by Christoph Knoch; **212** Titian, *Portrait of Pope Paul III*, c. 1543. Oil on canvas, 113.7 × 88.8 cm (44 ⅞ × 35 in.). National Museum of Capodimonte, Naples. Photo Scala, Florence; **215** *Backs and Fronts* (detail), 1981. Oil on linen and canvas, 243.8 × 609.6 cm (96 × 240 in.). Private collection. Image courtesy Magonza. Photograph by Michele Alberto Sereni;

219 *Mexico Vallarta 12.83*, 1983. Watercolour on paper, 22.9×29.2 cm (9×11½ in.). National Gallery of Art, Washington, DC, USA. Gift of Jane P. Watkins; **220** *3.29.84*, 1984. Watercolour on paper, 22.9×30.5 cm (9×12 in.). National Gallery of Art, Washington, DC, USA. Gift of Jane P. Watkins; **222** *Traveller 2.84*, 1984. Watercolour on paper, 22.9×29.2 cm (9×11½ in.). National Gallery of Art, Washington, DC, USA. Gift of Jane P. Watkins; **223** *Mexico 4.5.88*, 1988. Watercolour and pencil on paper, 30.5×40.6 cm (12×16 in.). Private collection; **225** Liliane Tomasko, London, 1995; **226** *Because of the Other*, 1997. Oil on linen, 243.8×365.8 cm (96×144 in.). Private collection; **227a** *Wall of Light Pink*, 1998. Oil on linen, 274.3×304.8 cm (108×120 in.). Museum of Fine Arts Boston, Boston, Massachusetts, USA. Museum purchase with funds donated by the Catherine and Paul Buttenwieser Fund and Davis and Carol Noble; **227b** *Wall of Light White*, 1998. Oil on linen, 243.8×274.3 cm (96×108 in.). The Metropolitan Museum of Art, New York, USA. Gift of Ginny Williams, 2007; **229** *Wall of Light Desert Night*, 1999. Oil on linen, 274.3×335.3 cm (108×132 in.). Modern Art Museum of Fort Worth, Fort Worth, Texas, USA. Collection of the Modern Art Museum of Fort Worth, Museum purchase. Photographed by Tom Powel Imaging. Courtesy Mnuchin Gallery; **230** *Planes of Light*, 1999. Oil on linen, 243.8×213.4 cm (96×84 in.). IVAM, Institut Valencià d'Art Modern, Valencia, Spain; **231** 'Painting', 2004. Ink on paper, dimensions unknown. Private collection. Photograph by Sean Scully Studio; **233** *Between Two Lights*, 1999. Oil on linen, 243.8×274.3 cm (96×108 in.). Private collection; **234** *Four Large Mirrors*, 1999. Oil on linen, 274.3×243.8 cm (108×96 in.) each. Kunstsammlung Nordrhein-Westfalen, Düsseldorf, Germany; **237** *Any Questions*, 1984–2005. Oil on linen, 259×324 cm (102×127½ in.). Private collection. Photograph by Trevor Good; **238** *The Bather*, 1983. Oil on linen, 243.8×304.8 cm (96×120 in.). Private collection. Photograph by Trevor Good; **241** 'Ellen', 2016. Ink on paper, 27.9×21.6 cm (11×8½ in.). Private collection. Photograph by Sean Scully Studio; **243** Scully family, 2014; **244** *Land Sea Sky*, 1999. Chromogenic print, 101.6×72.4 cm (40×28½ in.). Private collection

Acknowledgments

Thanks must first go to Sean Scully, without whose friendship, eloquence, generosity and trust this book could not have come about. I'm grateful too to Liliane and Oisin for allowing me to pull Sean away for so many marathon conversations during the spring and summer of 2020. Sincerest thanks are also owed to Roger Thorp, Thames & Hudson's extraordinary Editorial Director, whose vision is responsible for conceiving this book. I am extremely grateful too to the remarkable team at T&H for the care it has taken over the editing, design, production and promotion of the book. Finally, my deepest gratitude goes to my wife, Sinéad, and to our little boy, Caspar, for the boundlessness of their love.

Index